Praise for

Love's Work

"In its emphasis on the work of living, suffering, and loving, this is a masterpiece of the autobiographer's art, intense and rationally decorous at the same time."   —Edward Said

"*Love's Work* makes whatever else has been written on the deepest issues of human life by the philosophers of our time seem intolerably abstract and even frivolous."   —Arthur Danto

"This small book contains multitudes. It provokes, inspires, and illuminates more profoundly than many a bulky volume . . . and it delivers what its title promises, a new allegory about love."
                    —Marina Warner, *London Review of Books*

"This is an autobiography of astonishing elegance and concision. It is also deeply lyrical; a love song and a work song."   —Michael Wood

Love's Work

Love's Work

A Reckoning with Life

GILLIAN ROSE

SCHOCKEN BOOKS
New York

All rights reserved under International and Pan-American Copyright
Conventions. Published in the United States by Schocken Books Inc.,
New York. Distributed by Pantheon Books, a division of Random House,
Inc., New York. Originally published in 1995 in hardcover in Great Britain
by Chatto & Windus Limited, London, and subsequently in the United States
by Schocken Books, New York.

*Grateful acknowledgment is made to the following for permission
to reprint previously published material:*

Farrar, Straus & Giroux, Inc.: "Prayer to My Mother" from *Selected Poems* by
Pier Paolo Pasolini, translated by Norman MacAfee with Luciano
Martinengo; this English translation © 1982 by Norman MacAfee.
Reprinted by permission of Farrar, Straus & Giroux, Inc. • *Peters Fraser &
Dunlop Ltd.*: Excerpt from *The Wicked Pavilion* by Dawn Powell (W.H. Allen,
1954). Reprinted by permission of Peters Fraser & Dunlop Ltd. • *A. P. Watt
Ltd.*: Excerpts totalling 26 lines of poetry by William Butler Yeats.
Reprinted by permission of A. P. Watt Ltd.

Library of Congress Cataloging-in-Publication Data

Rose, Gillian.
Love's work: a reckoning with life / Gillian Rose.
p.   cm.
ISBN 0-8052-1078-4
1. Rose, Gillian. 2. Philosophers—England—Biography.
I. Title.
B1649.R74A3 1996
192—dc20 95-24358 [B]

Book design by Deborah Kerner

Printed in the United States of America
First American Paperback Edition
2 4 6 8 9 7 5 3 1

Keep your mind in hell,
and despair not.

STARETZ SILOUAN,
1866–1938

Love's Work

1

My first meeting with Edna was inauspicious.

It was May 1991. I had just arrived in New York for the first time in five years, and had been met at Newark Airport in New Jersey by Jim. Unsure of what to expect, I first walked up at the barrier to the wrong man—to someone who looked like a caricature of Jim as I remembered him in good health: well over six foot tall, a mane of blue-black hair, thickset, welcoming. Suddenly aware of my wilful mistake, I stopped just short of an inept embrace. I stood my ground and then I saw him. His posture was as crumpled as the clothes he'd obviously slept in, his hair had turned gingerish and it rose from his head in wild clumps with bald patches in between. This uneven growth dominated his manners, too, as I realised after one minute in the taxi heading towards Manhattan, which loomed in archetypal and mocking splendour ahead of us. My formerly laconic and witty friend had become loquacious, needy, addressing with urgent familiarity everyone we chanced to have dealings with over the next few days—taxi-drivers, bell-boys, waiters. And when he wasn't holding forth to those nearest to him, he issued a continuous, low, moaning sound, a piteous cradling for the inner, wounded being that, strangely, had surrendered to the publicity of the city streets. On Broadway, from Columbia University, where Jim's apartment was located on 111th Street, down to the Lincoln Center, where I went early morning swimming, I soon learnt to recognise multitudes like him:

the old men in their forties, shrivelled, drained, mumbling across the intersections, icons of AIDS, amidst the bodiful vibrancy of those striding to and from work and subways and stores.

By the time we reached Edna's apartment on West End Avenue, I was assailed by even more apprehensions. I felt uncomfortable meeting the two people who were offering me accommodation for the first time in the company of this unkempt and erratic being—my beloved friend—to visit whom was, I then thought, the whole purpose of my trip.

I needn't have worried, for each successive encounter proved as bizarre in its own way as the first. Gary, Edna's employer, was waiting in the foyer of 365 West End Avenue. I had been told that he was a private scholar, a man of means and intellect, meticulous and courteous. So he was: but I had not been told that he was afflicted with a long-term wasting disease that left him with uneven gait and hands locked in a rictus-like claw. Gary was utterly unfazed by Jim's doleful appearance and low-pitched litany, for he was only too eager to communicate the essentials concerning Edna in the short space of time we would have between leaving the lobby and reaching her fifth-floor apartment via the elevator. I knew that Edna was Gary's secretary and was expecting a dapper, matronly woman, perhaps in her fifties. Edna, Gary hurriedly explained, was ninety-three years old. She had recently contracted cancer of the face; and, as a result of a prosthetic jaw, had had to relearn to speak. When I then handed Gary the litre of Laphroaig purchased at Duty Free, he exclaimed, "Please God, you're not bearing whisky as a gift for Edna!" In her eighties, Edna had secretly started drinking a bottle of Calvados every day, until she had had to be hospitalised, detoxified and warned that her octogenarian life was at risk from her newly acquired habit. Thus we were ushered into Edna's presence and, increasingly confused, I met my Intelligent Angel for the first time.

Edna took Jim on, greeting and welcoming us both as her immediate "Darlings," in a rasping but emphatic voice. She settled us into her huge high-backed armchairs, a legacy, she explained, of the out-size men in her family. In this family, it turns out, there are no surviving men, just Edna, her sixty-eight-year-old retired mathematician daughter and her two granddaughters. Edna was diminutive amongst the heavy and ornate furniture; her tiny, wrinkled round face dominated by a false nose, which lacked any cosmetic alleviation whatsoever. Smooth and artificially flesh-coloured, with thick spectacles perched on top, this proboscis could have come from a Christmas cracker. In the early mornings, when I emerged from my room on my way to swim, Edna would have already been installed in her reading chair for an hour or two. She would call out to me to enquire whether I would mind if she were not to put on her nose. By then, not only did I not notice the nose, but, if anything, I found the neat, oblong black hole in her face even more appealing.

Edna goes out to work for Gary seven days a week, taking the bus uptown, but often walking the thirty or so blocks back downtown. She acts as Gary's hands, word-processing his scholarship and correspondence; he in turn acts as the guardian of her much less infirmities, lending support to her arm as they climb the stairs to the restaurant on Broadway and 112th Street where they take lunch daily.

Meeting this third extraordinarily afflicted person within the first hour of arriving in New York transformed the difficulties of the first two meetings. Edna and Jim were soon exchanging stories from New York music life. "I've taken part in New York music life since 1904," mused Edna. She would have been seven years old then. And I watched, not for the last time, the delight that flew between the fading forty-seven-year-old and the one full of ninety-three years.

Later, when I found myself alone with Edna, there were certain things which she was determined to make clear: "My marriage was not happy. My husband was disappointed with me. Although, when he died," she added, without a hint of triumph or rancour, "I was the only person permitted to attend him. The nurses in the hospital had to assure him that they were 'Edna.'" And for good measure, she also insisted that she did not eat vegetables. Nor, as she showed me around the apartment and we entered her bedroom, had she painted the room pink as long as her husband was alive: "I don't want you to think that I made a man sleep in a pink room."

Edna believes in magic. One of the many books that she handed over to me after her early morning reading sessions was *The Secret Garden* by Frances Hodgson Burnett. And the magic in that book is, I think, the kind of magic which Edna believes in: the quiet and undramatic transmutation that can come out of plainness, ordinary hurt, mundane maladies and disappointments. Thus she lives, while Jim, locked in a fatal embrace with maternal dreams, "where everything," he groaned, in one of his rare moments of lucidity, "begins with 's'"—his mother's name was *Esther*—Jim had to die.

What Edna did not tell me then, did not tell me until several years later, after her ninety-sixth birthday, when Jim was long dead and my own circumstances had radically changed, was that she had first been diagnosed as having cancer when she was sixteen years old—in 1913. She graduated from Barnard College in 1917. How can that be—that someone with cancer since she was sixteen exudes well-being at ninety-six? Could it be because she has lived sceptically? Sceptical equally of science and of faith, of politics and of love? She has certainly not lived a perfected life. She has not been *exceptional*. She has not loved herself or others unconditionally. She has been able to go on getting it all more or less wrong, more or less all the time, all the nine and a half decades of the present century plus three years of the century before.

Now, of course, I believe that it was Edna whom I went back to New York to meet. Edna was Jim's parting gift to me. She is an annunciation, a message, very old and very new. Edna is, as she insists, my "home from home." Whereas the idea of the original home would arouse an agon of bitter ambivalence in me, the redoubled home has no colour or cathexis of pain inseparable from its welcome.

2

My journey to Auschwitz and east across Galicia to Bełżec on the border of the Ukraine did not affect me in the ways I had expected: it was the unexpected, rather, which provided the nodes of enigma that compressed incompatible and uncomprehended meanings together.

In my inaugural lecture as Professor of Social and Political Thought at Warwick in February 1993, I mentioned that I was one of a number of Jewish "intellectuals" chosen to advise the Polish Commission on the Future of Auschwitz. What vain posturing! Scientific status, superimposed on the even more dubious notions of cerebral and cultural ethnic identity! We were set up. Enticed to preen ourselves as *consultants*, in effect, our participation was staged. Conscripted to restructure the meaning of "Auschwitz," we were observed rather than observing, the objects of continuous Holocaust ethnography, of Holocaust folk law and lore.

On the train from Warsaw to Kraków, from the comfort of the first-class compartment, my attention was drawn to a man who stood all the way in the corridor. Tall and angular, with a gaunt, beak-like visage, he seemed to bear accumulated suffering with majesty, as if generations of poverty and loss had pared away all excess to reveal without guise his true nature.

At the banquet held several days later in the baroque ballroom of the Grand Hotel of Kraków, once the favourite venue for Jewish wedding receptions, the evening was framed by the pastel stuccoed ceiling, tessellated floor and massive console mirrors. Gathered with our Polish counterparts, local dignitaries and intellectuals, we were served ample vodka to mask the absence of substantial food, in misplaced deference to the kosher scruples of the Jewish group. I found myself next to the intriguing stranger from the train. I discovered that he was a former aristocrat, like a large number of the assembled company, many of whom had spent the last forty years as art historians and curators, appointed custodians of their dispossessed familial palaces and mansions, with their sombre galleries of art and furniture.

My half-week in Poland had already taught me that I was in a land of martyred people, which harbours in its midst a still more martyred people—the Jews. No—the Jews are not *harboured*, but expelled into the borderless cemetery in the air, for the soil of death camps is cursed not consecrated ground, according to Halachah, Jewish law. From the tower of the Mariacki Church on the Rynek Głowny, the largest market square in Europe, on to which the hotel abutted, night and day, on every hour, the air vibrates with the plangent tones of the trumpeter. The trumpeter's long note, followed by two shorter notes of even lower pitch, to alarm the city of the enemy's advance, stops abruptly as the Tartar arrow pierces his neck. Four times, once to each corner of the tower, this herald of martyrdom doles out his fatal music, so that, wherever you are, you hear the foreboding and fading echo of his remorseless courses of ruin. As I travelled across the country, I learnt that it is this ever-repeated martyrdom that serves as the calibration of daily clock time, broadcast at noon every day on the radio station.

I found it more congenial to respond to Polish suffering: I found no consolation of lamentation for the Jews. In the beech forests outside Tarnów, where 800 children and 1,000 old and infirm Jews were shot, the roughly marked mass graves are surrounded, mid-March, by masses of tiny white wood anemones, wind-flower and bird-song, and the audibly rising sap of the pearly trees, as if a fairy tale has taken place here. At the desolation of Bełżec, the first death camp, there were no survivors, and there are no visitors today, just the freight trains thundering by in loud, rhythmic indifference. Nothing grows from this soil because 600,000 bodies were burnt out on the ground, which remains spongy with colourless grasses: nature is a death's head here. Six matt Soviet urns brood on the periphery of the camp, beyond which stretch spinneys of silver birches—the fairy fantasia even dares to hover on this horizon, too.

But I wept, I wept soft Polish tears for Count Potocki, not knowing, then, who he was. Later the same evening of the banquet, two colleagues and I were wandering around the centre of Kraków, looking for a tavern that had been recommended to us. Suddenly we found ourselves by mistake in a courtyard in the presence of the ailing Count. We had stumbled into his old family town house, which he had just recovered after forty years. He invited us to share a glass of tea with him, and conducted us up a solid central stairwell with a cast-iron balustrade, which, he explained, had been installed by the Nazis, to the top floor, where he inhabited two small rooms crammed full of furniture, largely covered with dust sheets. George Wheeler, one of my companions, conservation consultant from the Metropolitan Museum in New York, was qualified to relish the magnificence of such casually strewn antiques, while I noticed the sadness of the Count and the many pills he was swallowing. His sons, he said, would now return from the States to enjoy their patrimony, and his grandchildren would run gleefully up and down the stairs. The second floor of the house, he told us, as he carefully poured the tea from the awkward teapot, had been the art gallery, where the family's collection of paintings had hung, "The third largest private collection in Europe." The collection has been the property of the state since 1945, and is now housed in the main public gallery in Warsaw. He spoke without rancour, indeed without emphasis, in his perfect English. He had been a pupil at Ampleforth School in North Yorkshire, and had scraped a living for the past forty years as a translator from English to Polish. One thing he respectfully bade me do, aware, I now believe, but without humiliating me, of my ignorance of Polish history and hence of his lineage, was to read Adam Zamoyski's *The Polish Way*. And that was how, much later, I discovered who he was.

Eventually, we wished him good-night and began to descend the massive flights of stairs. The climb up had audibly shortened his breathing and he apologised for not accompanying us down and out into the polluted night air of Kraków. He remained stationed at the top of the stairwell, leaning on the heavy balustrade and watching silently as his visitors made their way down. It took an eternity to retraverse that Nazi monument, and he didn't take his eyes from us.

Was he remembering his wife, who had not lived to enjoy the return? Or anticipating the excited cries of his grandchildren? Or thinking back over the history of Poland, in which his ancestors had played so many decisive parts—as politicians, diplomats, poets and artists, and, above all and always, as owners of large estates worked by serfs? Yet I wept for this ruined and restored Pole—to my surprise, for I understood perfectly well that this reallocation of private property is designed to create a species of investment, to lure capital back from the States and from elsewhere in the diaspora. Such investment will finally demote limitless aristocratic seeming to the limits of bourgeois effecting and procuring.

"*Heschel'er Riddell Kalasheen Bandit.*" I love the sputter and beat of these words, with the accent falling on the ultimate syllable: Heschel'ér Riddéll Kalashéen Bandít. This was the curse my paternal grandmother would hurl at her husband when she was angry with him. She had frequent cause to be angry. She underwent fifteen pregnancies between 1899 and 1918, eleven live births, two babies smothered accidentally in her bed, and innumerable abortions. To this day, my father is not sure whether Mrs Pollock, who visited regularly once a year, was the midwife or the abortionist: the moans and shrieks from behind closed doors were such a regular season of family life. "Heschel'er" is the Yiddish diminutive for "Heschel," "Harry"—if you must. "Riddell," the family surname, changed hopefully to "Stone" to improve the family's Lancashire credentials. "Kalasheen" is the Yiddish version of Kalisz, the mid-Polish city from which the paternal family originates. "Bandit" is international: it means "You bandit!"

My father tells this story with obsessive relish, repeating his mother's words and rhythm. They suggest an almost saving humour: "You are incorrigible, but I must love you." By comparison, in my mother's family I find only devastation, made doubly demonical and destructive by the diversion of vast amounts of psychic energy devoted to its denial. Yet, when we were children, we were inducted without preliminaries into the mysteries. My mother said, "Grandma would kill German babies." "Why would Grandma kill German babies?" "Because the Germans killed Jewish babies."

My mother was brought up by a woman—her

mother, my grandmother—who was the only surviving member of her family. When Grandma was nineteen and Grandpa seventeen years old, they had run away from Łódź, also in mid-Poland, to Germany to marry, against the wishes of their families which belonged to different communities, Misnagdic and Hasidic. After their marriage, they followed Grandpa's family and emigrated to London. Between August 1939, when she and my grandfather last holidayed, as they did annually, in Łódź, and 1949, when Cousin Gutta came and told my grandparents that she, a remote cousin, was the only one left, fifty members of Grandma's family were killed—the children bayoneted first in front of their parents. Nowadays, my mother denies this; she denies that it happened and she denies that her mother suffered from it, so deep is her own unresolved suffering. This denial and unexamined suffering are two of the main reasons for her all-jovial unhappiness—the unhappiness of one who refuses to dwell in hell, and who lives, therefore, in the most static despair.

My God-forsaken families—from Kalisz and Łódź to Treblinka, but also to the East End of Manchester, Cheetham Hill Road, and to the East End of London, Whitechapel Road.

3

Yvette and I planned to visit
Jerusalem together, where she was born and
grew up. I very much wanted to go to Israel
with Yvette, who was teaching me biblical
and modern Hebrew, capital and cursive

script. But she died before we could realise our dreams.

Once I arrived late for a taxi at Yvette's flat in Harrington Road, Brighton. The flat was perched high above a vociferous fire-escape, which I always tried to dampen on ascending in order to surprise her. On this occasion I'd booked the taxi to fetch me from her place, since I wanted to deliver a volume to her and then fly on somewhere else. My mind went completely blank when the impatient driver remarked blandly, "There was an old woman at the address you gave me. She didn't know nothing about a taxi." An "old woman"? Who? Yvette? Preposterous!

While I copied out Rilke's *Elegies* for Yvette, Yvette sent me Yeats's "John Kinsella's Lament for Mrs Mary Moore":

> *None other knows what pleasures man*
> *At table or in bed.*
> What shall I do for pretty girls
> Now my Old Bawd is dead?

I suppose Yvette's looks could be misleading, for she was canny and crafty enough to disappear into the environment when it suited her purpose. From the moment that, unobserved, I first noticed and watched her, as she paced up and down the platform at Preston Park Station in Brighton, I knew that I was in the presence of a superior being. Green tights, a shapeless dark skirt and a mop of nondescript grey hair were but transparent media for the piercing intelligence in evident amused communication with itself, and warranting, on each turn at both ends of the platform, a grim but irrepressible smile, which spread slowly over her bare, unmade-up, delicate features.

This lucid apparition came to me many times—crossing the Level in Brighton, in the corridors of the School of European Studies, as well as frequently at that same station platform—before I found myself being introduced to her at Julius Carlebach's home, and the supernatural being began to acquire a measure of the natural.

That evening at Julius's was memorable for another reason. It was the occasion of my initiation into the anti-supernatural character of Judaism: into how *non-belief in God* defines Judaism and how change in that compass registers the varieties of Jewish modernity. The more liberal Judaism becomes, the less the orientation by Halachah, the law, and the greater the emphasis on individual faith in God. Julius sat at the head of the table in a dining-room which was museum and mausoleum of the Carlebach family's distinguished and dreadful history. Portraits of his ancestors presided. Between Solomon Carlebach, Rabbi of Lübeck, Julius's grandfather, mentioned in Thomas Mann's *Dr Faustus*, and Julius's cousin, Shlomo Carlebach, the singing Rabbi of Manhattan's Upper West Side, Julius's father, Joseph Carlebach, the famous Rabbi of Hamburg, accompanied his congregation from Hamburg to their death outside Riga, with his wife and the four youngest of their nine children. The square in Hamburg where his synagogue stood has recently been renamed Carlebach Platz. In his acceptance speech in Hamburg, when Julius received the honour on behalf of his family, he pointed out to his audience that they were assembled in the same school hall where he had stood, a fifteen-year-old schoolboy, on 10 November 1938, the day after *Kristallnacht*, when the Gestapo came and told the children that they had four weeks to leave Germany. "You could hear people collapse internally," Julius commented on his adult audience. What happened to those children?

At dinner, Julius explained, "An Orthodox Jew doesn't have to worry about whether he believes in

God or not. As long as he observes the law." Subsequently, I became familiar with the notoriously inscrutable Midrash: "Would that they would forsake Me, but obey my Torah." When we parted that evening, Yvette and I had agreed that I would visit her.

Yvette's dowdy and unselfconscious bearing was unable to conceal her visceral vocation as the Lover— not the Beloved: she was predator not prey. I had picked this up immediately that first time I spied on her from my station hide-out. The main room of her small granny-flat was furnished so that it conjured the atmosphere of Jerusalem's Ben Yehuda Street. Teeming with colourful artifacts, against the backdrop of the holy city, it re-created in miniature the bazaars of Eastern Europe, displaying the wares of so many destroyed folk cultures. From every available space, photographs of Yvette's five children and ten grandchildren listed tenderly towards her. We invariably sat opposite each other at the solid table by the window, high above the tree-lined road, and Yvette expounded to me her philosophy of love. Yvette was sixty-five years old when I first began to get to know her, and she had, concurrently, three lovers:

What lively lad most pleasured me
Of all that with me lay?
I answer that I gave my soul
And loved in misery,
But had great pleasure with a lad
That I loved bodily.

Flinging from his arms I laughed
To think his passion such
He fancied that I gave a soul
Did but our bodies touch,
And laughed upon his breast to think
Beast gave beast as much.

When I protested at this ceremony of lust, Yvette's reply was prepared: Yeats's "Last Confession" was elaborated by Swinburne:

No thorns go as deep as a rose's,
And love is more cruel than lust.

Yvette described my idea of creative closeness in relationships as a "total" and, by implication, totalitarian atittude. However, she insisted that while the number of her former lovers was too great to count, she had only been in love five times. This was an important distinction to her, and she appreciated having it confirmed by Miriam, her youngest child and only daughter.

Yvette was formidably well read. She had been married to an academic who taught English at the Open University, but now, in the mid-1980s, she was working as a secretary at the University of Sussex. Yvette regularly attended lectures and conferences, and she always posed with studied diffidence the most well-aimed critical questions, which presupposed her command of whatever literature was at stake. She was, however, deeply Francophile, and her staples were Proust—she reread *A la Recherche* in its entirety, once a year, in her antique, slightly foxed Pléiade edition— and Maupassant, all the passages and stories expurgated from school editions. She also had a sly but ardent passion for the novels of Ivy Compton-Burnett. And these authors, whom she inhabited, knowing them to be both enticing and rebarbative, were the source and confirmation of her philosophy of human relationships.

One Sunday, with the rain singing out of the secular silence, I met Yvette by chance walking in the unusually deserted Preston Park. We recognised each other with pleasure from afar. Yvette came up close to

me and put her hand on my arm. I already knew that
her daughter, Miriam, after years of not being able to
conceive, including an ectopic pregnancy, with the
consequent loss of one of her fallopian tubes, was now,
at long last, expecting. Yvette said in a factual and
unemotional tone of voice, "I have cancer of the breast.
I have to wait for an operation." She paused to gauge
my response, which was guided by her evident dispas-
sion, and then she added, "Miriam and I are now two
ladies-in-waiting."

Yvette was divorced from her husband. It had
been he who had initiated the decisive break after they
had had five children together. Yvette stressed that the
shock of their unanticipated separation did not derive
from the closeness of their tumultuous family life, but
from the fact that their partnership had always sus-
tained much extra-marital activity on both sides.
Several small children would be deposited in the cop-
ing hands of Nanny as Yvette snatched a furtive and
hurried rendezvous with her current liaison. "I loved
my man," she would defiantly assert of her former husband. Although she felt that she and her daughter
Miriam, in particular, had been utterly deserted by
him, she refused to rewrite history. Coming from
a family in which my mother divorced both of her

husbands, and, in addition, denied that she ever loved them, I found Yvette's aggressive vulnerability refreshing.

Yvette was the most enthusiastic and inventive grandmother. She couldn't spend enough time with her grandchildren, and she was especially close to Miriam's two children, who lived downstairs in the main body of the spacious Victorian house that Yvette had bequeathed to her daughter. She frequently visited her favourite son and his wife in Southampton with their older children. Another son would visit from London with his Sephardi wife and their two children, and the remaining two sons lived in Israel and Australia.

Yvette was completely devoted to pleasure without guilt. This was what made her such an attentive and encouraging confidante. She would listen with rapt attention to my confessions of pain and rage, but invariably dismiss my scruples, overcoming the nihilism of the emotions by affirming the validity of every tortuous and torturing desire. Although I was thus tutored by her, I watched with squeamish propriety as Yvette playfully squeezed her three-year-old grandson's balls and penis. "Aren't children meant to emerge to independence with a residue of resentment from the fact that it is the mother who accidentally arouses but explicitly forbids genital pleasure?" I ventured with theoretical pedantry in remembrance of Freud, and of the narrow border between child care and child abuse. Yvette positively relished my staid inhibitions, which she dismissed airily as contrary to the universal and sacred spirit of lust. A Grand Mother indeed.

In the far, dark corner of Yvette's main room there stood a heavy veneered chest of drawers with a pride of family photographs jostling on top. The three bottom compartments of this tallboy were jammed full with pornographic material, which, one day, after I'd known her for quite a while, Yvette showed to me. The photographs were almost entirely of women, clad in enough to titillate, and revealing proud genitals in various *contrapposto* positions. Yvette possessed very little male pornography, not because it is less available, but because it didn't interest her.

When I remarked one day, in a different context, that I couldn't reconcile her grandmotherly identity with her prodigious sexuality, she looked sadly and wisely at me as the one corrupted by unnatural practices: "Have you forgotten the connection between sex and children?" She was, of course, partly right.

Yvette's inexhaustible animus could be traced to her unsentimental disapproval of her own mother, as a mother and as an Israeli. According to Yvette, her mother, now in her nineties and living in a home in Jerusalem, had barred her children from loving or esteeming their father. Yvette's infinite fury at this ban had bestowed on her the lifelong celebration of lustful love. This vocation was inseparable from the rage at her mother, but also, and deeper still, it was insepar-able from her secret concurrence with her mother concerning the intellectual inferiority of the male. Her contempt was overlaid, and therefore indis-cernible to the untrained eye, with a much more explicit contempt for the resentful ruses of preyed-upon females.

To capture her distance from her mother as an Israeli, Yvette gives over the narrative voice to her for the space of a story. Yvette had, after all, run away in her early twenties with a one-legged Englishman, a "goy," as she would say. I cannot find a published ver-sion of this jumble tale, but one probably exists in Hebrew or Yiddish.

A LEGEND ABOUT THE BAAL SHEM TOV (BESHT)— THE BEARER OF A GOOD NAME

In the remote Polish village where he lived, there is a widow— shall we call her Katrilevska for she is not Jewish. She has several mouths to feed and is hopeless and helpless. A coarse-looking peasant enters her hovel and ascertains her needs. First, he brings her firewood, fills up her stove and lights it. Then he goes back, returning with two pails of water on his shoulders and now she can boil some coffee. Lastly he brings her a warm loaf. All this at 4 a.m., and all the while the peasant hums a song in a foreign tongue, but it is very sweet. He bids her farewell and disappears. It is the Besht, and he was humming tehilim, *and was back in his house just after 4 a.m., in time to pray* shakhrit.

The crucial thing is that Yvette's mother recited this story with disapprobation—or, I wonder, was it heard with disdain by the young Israeli children?

Yvette had two major recurrences of cancer before she died. After the first, relatively minor operation, a nip in the breast, which she valiantly displayed to select visitors, and several courses of chemotherapy, Yvette fell *in love*—in love, according to her own criterion—hopelessly and helplessly in love. But no

Besht ever came to save her or even to console her. The object of this serious passion was thirty years her junior, a colleague of my generation. Clever, charming, promiscuous and superficial, he enjoyed Yvette's friendship, but was genuinely disconcerted by her remorseless ardour. Yvette was monstrous: she pursued him with myriad love letters, phone calls, messages pinned to his door, unsolicited visitations. I taunted her, "Yvette, if you were a man, your actions would be seen as gross harassment." On a later occasion, her violent blandishments unabated, I asked her, archly, what she would do with him, were he, miraculously, to succumb? Yvette replied without a fraction of hesitation, "I would chew him up and spit him out."

A whole generation of young women and men were bereaved by Yvette's death. She made new friends up to the end, and she gave people, young and old, her courage to face the terrors of desire in themselves and to ease off the unstable alleviation of attributing to the Beloved our desire for those terrors. She could impart this wisdom because it grew out of the folly that she was still endlessly contesting in herself. And the cure for an unhappy love affair was always the pleasures of the ensuing one.

Yvette practised the *ars moriendi*; I had long

known that she would. The day before she died, her spirit intact, she listened with a look of beatitude on her simplified face to the story that I had brought with me from Leamington Spa, where I had just moved, to the Brighton hospice, where she lay in a room that formed a hard crystal of light, exposed to the raucous and merciless spring. It was a love story, and when I had finished relating it to her, and had sat quietly with her for several hours, she finally spoke out of the suffused silence, "You are now going to leave." Then, in her own way, she gave me her blessing: "You know how I feel. You know how I feel. Nothing has changed. Nothing has changed. All the very best. All the very best." I bent over her and kissed her on the lips several times, her lips reaching mine each time before mine touched hers.

Among the many pieces of unlined file paper, cut into thirds and covered with Yvette's old-fashioned typewriting, I found another fragment of Swinburne:

From too much love of living,
From hope and fear set free,
We thank with brief thanksgiving
Whatever gods may be

That no man lives for ever,
That dead men rise up never;
That even the weariest river
   Winds somewhere safe to sea.

I believe that I did in some sense visit Israel with Yvette, that through knowing her, I somehow reached the soul of that land of blessings and curses.

New York. Auschwitz. Jerusalem. My three Cities of Death: where I have been drawn time and time again over the last five years. My dead, dead Jim. Yvette across her civil wars. My numbered but nameless dead in Poland. Dearest, doughty Edna.

These lives, these deaths, like mine, come to me on the analogy from Plato between *the soul* and *the city*: the souls across the century, and the cities across the centuries.

Taking afternoon tea in the local, balmy Sunday park, surrounded by complaisant and complacent young families, the shallow waters of the duck pond idling in front of us, my sister Jacqueline, who had been working on Sylvia Plath and Anne Sexton, took a deep breath and announced: "I've had enough of mad girls."

4

I was never an innocent child. I was
for ever accompanied by four wicked and
energetic Particles, secret and clever
companions, who never allowed me any
inhuman innocence of beginning, and who
kept me prodigiously busy. These imps were

called "Im," "A," "Di" and "Dys": "Im-migration,"
"A-theism," "Di-vorce," "Dys-lexia." Dyslexia, the last
of these genies, is really the first: for, by discovering
from very early on that the desert of stony words
could be made to bloom, that I could channel what I
could not overcome, I acquired a puckish strategy for
enchanting the agents of adversity. The fourth disabil-
ity could be made to germinate the other three.

In Jerusalem, Paul Mendes-Flohr's son, Itamar, is
so profoundly dyslexic that, at the age of twelve,
he cannot read a single word in any of the three languages which he speaks fluently: Hebrew, American-
English and Arabic. Rita, his mother, is a Sephardi Jew
from Curaçao, hence the "Mendes" in the family name.
His father, Paul, is an American Jew. Itamar bears
five names: his parents' amalgamated surname, and
three given names, one Israeli, one Arabic, one
English.

Itamar's parents, secular Zionists, are pro-
Palestinian and active in the peace movement. Rita, his
mother, architect and artist, stands daily in the roaring
midday sun, dressed in heavy, black, long garments,
with other women, mostly Ashkenazim, members
of the protest movement "The Black Palestinian
Women." They expect the insults hurled from

marauding bands of right-wing youths, who also con-
gregate in the square. Itamar's father, Paul, hosts a
group of Arab intellectuals and Israeli academics who
assemble weekly at the American Colony Hotel, situated between the Damascus Gate and Herod's Gate,
the one location in Arab East Jerusalem where you see
vehicles parked next to each other, some with Israeli
and some with Arab numberplates. Paul, who com-
bines his political activities with being Professor of
German-Jewish Intellectual History at the Hebrew
University, has lost the sight in one of his eyes by
neglecting to procure any treatment for a detached
retina.

Dyslexia in a Jewish child is fraught with signifi-
cance. For childhood is the preparation for the reading
of the portion of the law at thirteen, the bar mitzvah,
when the child becomes an adult, "a son of the law." In
Itamar's case, I suspect, as in mine, the inability to read
is a blind protestantism, an unconscious rebellion,
against the law, the tradition of the fathers, and against
the precipitous fortress of the family. The stuttering in
the face of the Written Word enacts a mimesis of the
embattled and shattered truth of father and family. The
confusion of names marks the child with the stigmata
of the fantasised identity which he cannot assume—

and so he stumbles against its central asylum, the written names of the law.

My conviction that I harboured secret, malign and crafty powers was encouraged by the adult treatment of me as a well wound-up mechanical toy that perversely refused to work. The emotional and symbolic meaning of my dyslexia was overlaid and obscured by several physical disabilities, which received a lot of attention.

Quite recently I was propelled out of an optician's chair with the impetus of primitive and long-forgotten despair, when the optician remarked to me casually that I have a "lazy" eye. On recovering my equilibrium and equanimity, I had it explained to me that the epithet "lazy" is employed to render the nature of a squint intelligible to children. I riposted that this vicious metaphor can only be heard by a child as a harsh, personal judgement on her very being, on her good intentions and on her willingness to collaborate. Since the defect in my vision and the defect in my comprehension of words on the page were not distinguished from each other, the pronouncement "lazy" tore down through me and made me determined, once I learnt to read, never to rest in the work of deciphering dangerous and difficult scripts.

The uncoupling of my wandering eye and my wandering mind did not finally occur until I was seven years old. I woke up in a hospital bed to find myself in the unaccustomed presence of both my father and my mother, which made me immediately aware, before I'd fully regained consciousness, that something very important and serious was happening to me. A row ensued between the two of them as to whether I should be permitted to eat or not. I cannot remember whose view prevailed, but I do remember being fed mashed banana, which I promptly vomited up. Meanwhile, the operation to correct the squint was successful, and now I could concentrate on learning to read.

Reading, however, did not interest me. With a persistent, dreary ache, my habit of sounding out words backwards, of not seeing sense in the unit of conjoint letters, gave me the dull conviction that I was a closed creature where reading was concerned. The special teacher, to whose house I was taken unwillingly every day after school, her voluminous, unified breast bolstered on the table next to the tall glass of cold milk and the plate of dry, predictable biscuits, did not seem a likely anagoge into recalcitrant mysteries which possessed only a dubious claim on my soul.

The only paradises cannot be those that are lost, but those that are unlocked as a result of coercion, reluctance, cajolery and humiliation, their thresholds crossed without calm prescience, or any preliminary perspicacity. Reading was never just reading: it became the repository of my inner self-relation: the discovery, simultaneous with the suddenly sculpted and composed words, of distance from and deviousness towards myself as well as others. My disastrous Judaism of fathers and family transmogrified into a personal, protestant inwardness and independence. Yet, as with the varieties of historical Protestantism, progenitor of modernity, the independence gained from the protest against illegitimate traditional authority comes at the cost of the incessant anxiety of autonomy. Chronically beset with inner turmoil, the individual may nevertheless become roguishly adept at directing and managing the world to her own ends. Little did I realise then how often I would make the return journey from protestantism to Judaism.

On my sixteenth birthday I changed my surname by deed poll from "Stone" to "Rose," from my

father's name to my stepfather's name. From one het-
eronym to another: for, if "Stone" substituted for
the Polish-Jewish "Riddell," then "Rose," English
Rose, masked German-Jewish "Rosenthal," valley of
roses, one of the many horticultural names arbitrarily
adopted on emancipation by a people whose God is
absent from nature. This violent act of self-assertion,
which was the culmination of several years of impatient waiting, served as my bat mitzvah, my confirmation as daughter of the law. It represented the end of
my legal childhood, during which the conditions of my
father's access had been established by frequently chal-
lenged Orders of the Court. Now *I* could decide on
the pattern of communication and on our "access" to
each other. My prematurely adult self-image was,
however, severely dented soon after this *rite de passage*.
I discovered, to my disgust, on personal supplication
for my birth certificate at the Public Record Office in
Chancery Lane in order to apply for my first passport
under my new name, that I was officially, in law, at the
age of sixteen—worldly, voluptuous and scholarly as I
fancied myself—an INFANT SPINSTER.

I did not, of course, control any of the conse-
quences of my action. My father responded rapidly to
my change of name by officially disowning me. As a

result, I did not see him between the ages of sixteen and twenty-one. The Name: the Name. A rose is [not] a rose is [not] a rose is [not] a rose. And it was Gertrude Stein who formulated the positive version of that liturgy—*Stein*, a "Stone," no less.

During a three-year period, when, a Lecturer at the University of Sussex, I was working on the German schools of neo-Kantianism, the dry and dusty volumes of epistemology evacuated from the entrails of the British Library, I purchased my first property. It was a modest, two-bedroomed flat in a character-less modern block with shaky foundations in Stoke Newington, the only part of London that I could afford. I worked three days a week in the British Library and commuted to Brighton on the other two. In Stoke Newington I gradually discovered that I was dwelling among a community of Hasidic Jews, the Lubavitch Habad. "Gradually discovered" because, while the men are instantly recognisable in their late eighteenth-century gaberdines, summer and winter, with their square beaver hats and long ringlets hanging down over each ear, flanking their pallid, earnest faces, it takes longer to identify the women and children. They have a superficial appearance of normality, which is all the more estranging in its radical deviation from the working-class norm, in this outer ring of London, to which the underground does not extend. On marriage, women belonging to this sect shave their heads, and from then on they wear a wig, called a *sheitl*, which means "parting," so named because of the parting, the line of absence of hair, in this lugubrious concession to the cosmetic. They bear a child annually, issue of the commandment to copulate every Sabbath eve, and to refrain during and after menstruation, when the women immerse themselves in the *mikveh*, the public ritual bath. The limbs of these children are completely covered up, arms and legs hidden by gravid garments, whatever the season or temperature of the air. At night I could imagine that I was a *flâneur* in Middle Europe: strains of High German, French and Italian, as well as Yiddish and Hebrew, would percolate from the street through the open windows of my flat. And on those days when, my own hair unwashed, I dashed to the launderette in the local parade of shops, with a chiffon scarf covering my head, my face scrubbed and unmade-up, I would be greeted and treated as a member. This involved cultivating a passing talent for altercation: arguing for priority in drying my linen, because *my* plane was leaving for the Holy Land half an hour earlier than the transport of my adversary.

I did not realise how deeply I had become accustomed to this neighbourhood iconography of the holy community, living in the midst of that peculiarly dense piety of popular Kabbalah, which enjoins the men—and only the men—to return the divine sparks to the creator in ritual song and dance, until one day, looking out of the window of the flat, I saw a wedding party arrive at the block of flats on the opposite side of the road. Not an Hasidic wedding, an ordinary English wedding. What struck me at once was the lightness of the vision: slender young bridesmaids in short white muslin dresses with loose bare limbs, the adults attired in the pastel hues of matrimonial finery, and the commingling of the sexes in easy high spirits, all on their way from the church ceremony to the jollifications of the reception. My disinterested perception of this happy procession was brusquely interrupted by the loud irruption of a subhuman howling, the source of which was unlocatable. It was howling as if from a dark, dank cave, where some deformed brute had been chained and tempted since time immemorial. The howling did not cease even after the last of the wedding party had disappeared from view.

It was I who was howling, in utter dissociation from myself, the paroxysm provoked by the vivacious contrast between the environing Judaism and this epiphany of protestants, the customary, laborious everydayness broken by the moment of marriage, the cloaks of the clandestine pious cleaved by the costumes of those weightless, redeemed beings. To this day, I cannot go to family weddings.

It was when I was living in Stoke Newington that I finally passed my driving test. I had to overcome not only the fundamental lack of co-ordination between my mind and the mechanics of the motor vehicle, but, I discovered here, too, a much deeper inhibition. I see in my mind's eye that no-man's-land which I had had to cross from the security of home, harbouring my mother, stepfather and sisters, to my father's car, parked and waiting at a tangent to the house. My sister and I, obliged by court to spend one weekend afternoon a fortnight with my father, would be driven somewhere by him for a few hours, usually to the cartoon cinema, situated in Terminal One at London Airport. The battles waged between my father and myself took place, however, in his mystical chariot. Wheels within wheels and full of dreadful eyes, the enthroned Almighty chastised his prophet Ezekiel for his abject rebellion. Sitting in the front passenger seat, I was wrathfully and precisely informed that I had broken the fifth commandment to honour (not *to love*, note) my father as well as my mother. Indeed, I had. Measured palm against his palm, fingers against his fingers, I was told that I was the bearer of hands with the magnitude of a man. I think my resistance finally broke one Saturday afternoon, when my father told me, by way of explaining my beloved stepmother's unusual absence, that it was my wickedness that had caused her to lose the child that she had been carrying—the little brother I so craved, living, as I did, in a world of sisters.

Court case after court case contesting the conditions of access followed these traumatising interviews. And, to my increasing horror, my devilish powers grew apace out of the demonising of my father. How many children find that their fear and hatred of a parent can actually land that parent in court, defending himself against charges brought on the child's initiative? What happens to children who split off their ambivalence about their parent and neatly personify it in two separate characters—the wicked father and the good stepfather? This long and perilous upbringing spoilt my imagination: my ability to distinguish between fantasy and reality, to be able to feel murderous in the confidence that I would never commit the foul act. It ruined my capacity to tolerate highly charged yet contrary emotions about the same person, and not to isolate the dangerous aspects exclusively in one real person.

This is the source of my excessive spirituality, my screwtape obsession with disembodied truth. How do I know what my father said to me? Over the years, I have asked him and my stepmother again and again whether they really did tell me that I was responsible in effect for the miscarriage of a foetus too immature for its sex to be formed. They always respond with great loving kindness, yet, and here's the rub, I can never remember what they reply to my mythical question. No matter how many times I ask them, and no matter how hard I try, I cannot recall the answer.

After one especially bitter court case, I learnt from Ann, our long-standing, resident mother's help and adopted member of the family, that the judge had pronounced: "A plague on both your houses." This surreptitious knowledge, smuggled in to me, of something not right on both sides, must have saved me by restoring a sense of unresolvable truth, by putting a disturbing and fuzzy paradox in the place of stern and unequivocal judgement. But to this day, I do not care to drive a car.

My overcharged gnostic imagination continues
to embellish the Manichaean opposition between my
fathers. Doctors of medicine, they are equally disaf-
fected Jews. I do not use the conventional term,
"assimilated," because it fails to capture the energetic
alienation from traditional Judaism which so forms the
modern Jew, and which accentuates adopted characteristics—the dour and abrasive Yorkshireman, the
horse-mad Irishman, full of the blarney.

On the two Passover *Seder* nights at my maternal
grandparents', in the interstices of the assembled company's chanting of the Hebrew, my father tenaciously
polices solecisms of grammar and pronunciation in the
halting conversations which take place between the
adults and the children in English with frequent lapses
into Yiddish. My grandparents, who move easily
between Yiddish, Polish, Russian, Hebrew and French
(the last of these languages specially acquired for their
frequent holidays at the gaming tables of Cannes and
Nice), are indifferent and heavily accented speakers of
English. They find my father's strictures burdensome
and offensive, and they persist in their macaronic med-
ley of tongues.

When my stepfather replaces my father at *Seder*
nights, the stakes are raised. In the place of a po-

liceman, we have a comedian. Irving intones the Haggadah in the dutifully monotonous mumble of a son of the law. The patriarch, my grandfather, presides at the head of the long table, laden with all the traditional signs and symbols. The youngest male child, my cousin, whose question, "Why is this night different from all the other nights?" begins the holy recital, sits on one side of him; the eldest female child, myself, who, at the appointed time, opens the front door for Elijah, so that the angel of death should pass over the house, sits on the other side of him. In the course of the service, which has its high points in the hide and seek of the coins in the matzo, but also its *longueurs*, Irving interjects into the steady flow of the Hebrew a stream of very Anglo-Saxon obscenities. Grandpa pretends not to hear and continues expressionless in his recitation. For the children, the exquisite pain begins of trying to suppress their hilarity. The acceleration of these depredations is as predictable as the order of the service itself. Grandpa starts to threaten disapproval by the most subtle expressions of discomfort, while the young people increasingly fail to suffocate their mix of consternation and glee at this wholesome transgression. Eventually—how long can we hold out?—Grandpa pauses and feigns long-suffering exasperation, the children collapse in merriment, and Irving makes a show of contrition.

The contrast between my father's strict, clipped conformity to the Queen's English and my stepfather's love of the underside of the language, pronounced with a Dublin lilt, gives you the difference of character and temperament: the stern eye versus the eye moist with humour and illicit pleasure; the one, doctor of medicine turned stockbroker, devoted to the professional accumulation of wealth, who gives nothing away; the other, doctor of medicine and compulsive gambler, reckless and profligate, who carelessly loses everything. The stone and the rose. In my thirties, as my elected apprenticeship in Judaism deepened, I approached my father and urged him to give me a five-volume set of the Bible with the Commentary of Rashi, the great medieval philosopher and Talmudist. I explained to him that it is traditional for a Jewish father to give the set of five volumes to his son. My sister Diana, who overheard my request, commented in a factual tone of voice, "Asking our father for something is like trying to get blood out of a stone." Nevertheless, he obtained the set for me and inscribed it with his blessing for his strange eldest daughter of the law, who takes the son's part, too. Irving brings me pink peonies, *Pfingstrosen*, Pentecostal roses, magnified blooms of the early summer harvest, the eternal in the fleeting benison.

O worship the King all glorious above;
O gratefully sing his power and his love;
our shield and defender, the Ancient of Days,
pavilioned in splendour and girded with praise.

O tell of his might, O sing of his grace,
whose robe is the light, whose canopy space;
his chariots of wrath the deep thunder-clouds form,
and dark is his path on the wings of the storm.

The earth with its store of wonders untold,
Almighty, thy power hath founded of old;
hath stablished it fast by a changeless decree,
and round it hath cast, like a mantle, the sea.

This contrary deity, among whose celestial architecture I so longed to dwell, did not deign to destroy me. I adored this hymn because it contained so many enticing words and constructions which I barely grasped:

"pavilioned," "whose canopy space." In order to possess these arcana, I stole the hymn book. I can still see the small, neat red book, nestling in the satchel which hung on the side of the chair of the child who worked next to me on the long table in the L-shaped schoolroom. I coveted that hymn book for a long time, although I knew that I was not meant to have one. I knew nothing else; for, at that stage, my being Jewish was as empty and inconvenient to me as having knock-knees and a squinting eye, impositions, which belonged, nevertheless, to the order of nature and necessity.

But the god betrayed me. I was found out: that was a relief. But the relief did not release me, because it was not completed by kind punishment or by any admonition whatsoever. I was let off. No one told me that I had done wrong to steal, but neither did anyone try to talk to me about why I had committed such a planned yet impetuous crime. Once the red hymn book had been restored to its rightful owner, the affair was simply overlooked. The outcome of such forbearance was not simple for me: it was wracking. It left me at the mercy of a guilt that I could not begin to expiate myself. I was forced into an inner thraldom to an unknown god, whose outer attributes and ener-

gies—"the earth with its store of wonders untold"—
had initially aroused in me a purely pagan delight in
his fastness, pavilioned in splendour, whose canopy
space; in his fullness of power and love, of might
and grace.

As an acolyte, I was not resourceless: the divorce,
already in harness to the dyslexia, came to the aid of
my unenlightened gnosticism. I became learned in the
sacred lexicons of the paternal dissimilitudes: the
stone and the rose.

Do you know what happens in the Australian film
of Peter Weir based on the novel by Joan Lindsay, *Picnic
at Hanging Rock*? Mesmerised by this haunting story,
people persist in posing its central mystery as a quest
for knowledge. Everyone wants to know what became
of the two schoolgirls and one of their teachers who
disappear for ever during a picnic at Hanging Rock on
St Valentine's Day in 1900. To me, it is obvious what
happens. I know because the central mythic opposition
in the story is that of the stone and the rose. The hanging rock is the Rock of Zion. It denotes a deity who is
removed from the natural world and who leaves no
tracks. Such a deity can only be alluded to by the most
implacable, impenetrable, and unarticulated manifestation of nature. Sublime and severe, the rock is

supremely dangerous; for it takes whatever it wants and offers no explanation. It is power and might without love and grace: the god of an old testament, the Ancient of Days.

To this rock come a band of virgins; the very young girls arrive at the rock, whose 350 million years already terrify them. At midday, when time stops, the knife slices the heart-shaped Valentine cake in half, proleptic penetration of their as yet intact vaginas, intactness which is monitored explicitly through the story. The girls are spring roses and romance; they are all articulateness, beauty, inwardness, passion and preoccupation with self-representation.

One girl stays behind: the orphan, Sara, who is driven to suicide after the picnic by the persecution of the headmistress, Mrs Appleyard. The school is ruined by the disappearing girls and the suicide; and Mrs Appleyard is impelled to throw herself from the rock at the end of the film and the book.

The story offers us no solace of psychology or melancholy, which we yearn to find in it. It presents the pattern of a doom and a consummation. Miranda, the most senior girl who disappears and whose namesake is the daughter of a sorcerer, is the seer: she foretells the future and leads the way. She is likened to "a

Botticelli angel" by Mademoiselle, the French teacher. This teacher is voluptuous and whole; engaged to be married, she will become the matriarch who survives to tell her grandchildren, the succeeding generations, the story of the picnic at the rock, unlike the middle-aged virgin mathematician, who climbs after the ascending girls and partakes in their perfecting.

Miranda guides the other three girls up the rock face. The doom of Sara is announced and the oracular judgement pronounced—"Everything begins and ends at exactly the right time and place"—before the girls begin to offer themselves, virgin sacrifice, to the male spirit of the voiceless rock. Taking off their sandals and stockings and loosening their girdles, they continue their ascent in silence. In the arrest of time, the fresh roses of light and love are turned into the sublime eternity of the aphonic stone. Sheer power and vulnerable passion are united in a mystic marriage, the marriage of power and might with grace and love, the Romance of the Rose in semi-modern dress.

What happened to them? They took and were taken into eternal life in exchange for the eternal damnation of Sara and Mrs Appleyard.

Sara, enamoured of Miranda, is the one child forbidden to attend the picnic; she and Mrs Appleyard, the headmistress, are doubles. It is a battle of will and wits between the powerful, persecuting head teacher and the poetic and vulnerable orphan, whose guardian leaves her without protection. The victim will not become good: she makes her own the violence that she is dealt, just as Mrs Appleyard is dominated by the abuse which damaged and deformed her. Their mirrored doom precipitates the action. These mythic characters are contrasted with characters who represent humanity and psychology, finite integrity and finite love: Mike, Sara's brother, by whose persistence one of the girls, Irma, is recovered, and Minnie and Tom, the school's servants and illicit lovers, who will marry and thrive.

What happened?—*divine retribution*, timeless and foreknown. Thus the order of the film, that it begins with the picnic and disappearance of the girls and ends with the two suicides, is of no consequence. The parity is the theme, for these mysteries balance each other, regardless of their temporal sequence: "Everything begins and ends at exactly the right time and place."

This clairvoyant exposition of the stone and the rose, whether the pagan version of sublime boulder and virgin-sacrifice, or the Judaeo-Christian version of

the Rock of Zion and the Romance of the Rose, con-
jures an egregiously erotic spirituality. It misrepresents
the meaning of repentance and redemption in Judaism
and in Christianity for the sake of the drama of their
iconography. My spoiled entrance to comparative religion invites me to luxuriate in these overripe inter-
pretations, even while the proud energy of the earnest
autodidact is being distilled into the cautious attention
of the theodidact.

These return journeys between protestantism
and Judaism defy any idea of "ethnic" identity. My
protestantism has been imbibed with the vapours of
the culture; my learning helps me to describe it. My
Judaism is cerebral and consciously learnt; it permits
me to develop a perspective on quandaries which
would otherwise remain amorphous and alien.

As my grandfather lay dying, he lapsed into High
German, a language which, like all German products
but German automobiles in particular, had been
banned from my grandparents' house and presence
since the war. Yet who would have thought the old
man to have had so much German in him? As with
most Polish Jews, Yiddish seemed his lingua franca.
Polish Yiddish is, of course, a combination of Middle
German with some Hebrew, written in Hebrew char-

acters. How did my grandfather acquire such perfect High German? As he lay there plucking at his heart, the forbidden words poured out of his mouth. I was the only close mourner who could understand what he was trying in his agitation to convey.

This was his final bequest: the very language into which I believed that I had safely alienated my adult vocation by becoming a scholar of German philosophy. I had taught myself German, which is a highly inflected language, by reading the works of T. W. Adorno. I was attracted by the ethical impulse of his thought, but also by the characteristics of his style, the most notoriously difficult sentence structure and the vocabulary full of *Fremdwörter*. This embarkation also betrays a further motivation: an inexorable inner need to experience my dyslexia in daily intercourse with the signs and syntax of Adorno's forbidding universe. Was this recalcitrant medium, whose rigours I had willingly assumed, a legacy, a return to ancestral tradition, and not, as I had thought, the channel for my protestantism against the broken promises of the mother-tongue?

5

However satisfying writing is—that mix of discipline and miracle, which leaves you in control, even when what appears on the page has emerged from regions beyond your control—it is a very poor substitute indeed for the joy and the agony of loving. Of

there being someone who loves *and* desires you, and
he glories in his love and desire, and you glory in his
ever-strange being, which comes up against you, and
disappears, again and again, surprising you with difficulties and with bounty. To lose this is the greatest loss,
a loss for which there is no consolation. There can only
be that twin passion—the passion of faith.

The more innocent I sound, the more enraged
and invested I am.

In personal life, people have absolute power over
each other, whereas in professional life, beyond the
terms of the contract, people have authority, the
power to make one another comply in ways which
may be perceived as legitimate or illegitimate. In personal life, regardless of any covenant, one party may
initiate a unilateral and fundamental change in the
terms of relating without renegotiating them, and
further, refusing even to acknowledge the change.
Imagine how a beloved child or dog would respond, if
the Lover turned away. There is no democracy in any
love relation: only mercy. To be at someone's mercy is
dialectical damage: they may be merciful and they may
be merciless. Yet each party, woman, man, the child in
each, and their child, is absolute power as well as
absolute vulnerability. You may be less powerful than

the whole world, but you are always more powerful than yourself.

Love in the submission of power.

I am highly qualified in unhappy love affairs. My earliest unhappy love affair was with Roy Rogers. I loved him so much that it caused me acute physical pain just to think of him, and the high point of every week was watching his programme on television. It was no coincidence that the programme was broadcast weekly on Saturday afternoons at exactly the time I was due, fortnightly, to see my father. Yet, this unabashedly aggressive love, intoxicated with defiance, was an achievement. Prior to its development, I had vomited every other Friday, ostensibly over the fried, breadcrumbed plaice to which the household was habituated for the sake of Ann, who was an Irish Catholic, but, virtually, in anticipation of the dreaded Saturday afternoons.

My desire to possess Roy Rogers for my love was inseparable from my equally unshakeable desire *to be* him: I wanted *to be* and *to have*. My mother set off to Harrods to purchase a cowboy outfit for me. She was stopped in her tracks when the toy department assistant routinely enquired, "How old is your little boy?" But I was not daunted and was busy anyway training myself to urinate from a standing position. My father was not amused. And in this exceptional case, my mother, for reasons of her own (her fear of my burgeoning gender proclivities), put an end to the affair, and so acted in my father's interest, too. She told me that, as an English female, the closest aspiration I could entertain to my ambition, not to grow up to be, but to assume immediately the life of a cowboy, was to become a *milkmaid*. The lot of Dale Evans, my erstwhile rival, was not to my liking. Heartbroken, I put away my two pistols in their plastic holsters with other childish things. I preferred to renounce my love fantasy altogether rather than embrace the reduced reality held out to me. Inauspicious beginning to the long, gruelling ordeals of love to come.

Happy love is happy after its own fashion: it discovers the store of wonders untold, for it is the intercourse of power with love and of might with grace. Nothing is foreign to it: it tarries with the negative; it dallies with the mundane, and it is ready for the unexpected. All unhappy loves are alike. I can tell the story of one former unhappy love to cover all my other unhappy loves—in particular, the one that is ruining me at present. The unhappiest love is a happy love that has now become unhappy.

I discovered that behind my early idealisation of men and dependence on them, there lurked a rage at having been deserted by my fathers, and at their having allowed my mother to dispose of them. Then I discovered the even more deep-seated corollary in the lack of independence of my carefully chosen current lover. I have observed in some of my women friends that their principled anger arising from the history of their oppression by father, husband, lover, covers up the deeper but unknown rage at the carefully chosen impotence of the current partner.

Down by the salley gardens my love and I did meet;
She passed the salley gardens with little snow-white feet.
She bid me take love easy, as the leaves grow on the tree;
But I, being young and foolish, with her would not agree.

In a field by the river my love and I did stand,
And on my leaning shoulder she laid her snow-white hand.
She bid me take life easy, as the grass grows on the weirs;
But I was young and foolish, and now am full of tears.

My first communication with Father Dr Patrick Gorman took the form of a request for some references concerning eighteenth-century German Pietism. Always fascinated by this reformation of the Reformation, I had been told that the new member of faculty, Catholic and Marxist though he was, was jesuitically well informed in the history and theology of the Protestant as well as the Catholic Counter-Reformation. Shortly afterwards, I found a typed list of scholarly references pinned to my office door. The note terminated with "We share students, we exchange notes, we have seen each other across a crowded room. Shall we not meet?" The romance of this guarded proposition was met with blankness on my part concerning which crowded room might have levelled our gaze—the refectory, the European School common room, the Arts Centre bar? I was sure that I had not set eyes on Father Dr Gorman.

Subsequently, I found myself in a routinely tedious faculty meeting, in which, as usual, I carried no presence whatsoever. As drivers insist that the blaring radio aids their concentration on the road, so I always found that a volume open on my lap enabled me to pay the small amount of attention needed to navigate these shallows. When asked with withering detection by the impassive secretary whether the book I was blatantly perusing was good, I nonchalantly

replied, "I only read good books." I responded simi-
larly to her policing my failure to send a note of
apology for a meeting that I actually managed to miss,
"But I'm not sorry." On this particular occasion, I was
aware of an intense aura emanating from someone
whom I had never seen before, an intense, sexual aura,
aimed precisely and accurately at my vacant being. "A
man," I wondered, "could there be a man in this meeting?" He looked weather-beaten, his flat, lined faced
suffused with a self-consciously alert intelligence and a
knowledge of sensual power. I had no idea who he
was, and did not pursue the matter.

One lunch hour, as I was hurrying purposelessly
across campus, *sine ira ac studio*, without anger or
enthusiasm, the perfect legal-rational bureaucrat
according to Max Weber, oblivious to my surround-
ings, a student importuned me on behalf of someone
who stood motionless a few feet away and who required my attention. As we shook hands, Father Dr
Patrick Gorman and the man in the meeting merged
alarmingly into the same person.

Does "love at first sight" mean that you fall in love
the instant you meet someone, or does *the first sight*
occur when you suddenly fall in love with someone
you may have met or known for any amount of time?

One evening, not long after that fortuitous dénouement, I was invited to dine with Patrick Gorman in his suite of perfectly proportioned eighteenth-century rooms adjoining the Church of St J———. When I arrived, Patrick was engaged on the telephone in the small lodge, already crowded with two of his colleagues. In a dark dinner suit surmounted by his white dog-collar, Patrick immediately gripped my hand and, looking me straight in the eye, did not release the tension between our clasped hands and locked eyes for the duration of the telephone call. While I swallowed hard to return the power of such a greeting, Patrick's confrères seemed unperturbed by their brother's ravishing reception of the scholarly young woman.

Time and time again that evening, it was I who encountered the limits of my prejudices and inhibitions, not he. Champagne was the only drink, and the food was an initiation into sensual rites in which I had not until then participated—oysters, turbot, lemon soufflé. Patrick converted me before the evening was over to a serious interest in Latin American Liberation Theology, an amalgam of Marxism and the Bible, which proved a most uneven body of literature. More significantly, he introducd me to its philosophical roots in the earlier transcendental Thomism of Rahner and Lonergan. In return, I persuaded him to deepen his Marxism by reassessing its relation to the works of Hegel; and, predictably, I introduced him to Rilke's *Sonnets to Orpheus*.

Patrick had a collection of recordings of Dietrich Fischer-Dieskau singing Schubert *Lieder*, which he had built up over twenty years. He observed, with the composed melancholy of one who knows the long travail and discipline of love, how Dieskau's renderings of Schubert have mellowed and matured over the decades. I observed to myself how the human face is a multiple sexual organ—orifices and protrusions, yeses and noes, nose and eyes and lip and ear. I should have taken more heed, when in reply to my note of thanks for the evening, Patrick cited Dante, *Paradiso*, Canto XVI, ll. 67–9:

> *Sempre la confusion de le persone*
> *principio fu del mal delle cittade,*
> *come del corpo il cibo che s'appone.*

(The confusion of persons is always the source of the evil of the city, as, in the body, when food is indigested.)

In the New Year, I went to spend a few days with

Patrick at St A—— in H——, Surrey, where he had
been allotted the parish while he was teaching at the
University of Southampton. His accommodation was
austere, while his manners remained as pagan as ever.
The bare boards, unshaded lamp and narrow bed in his
room, given over to me, were humble companions
to the lush crucifix and rank icon of the Virgin and
Child.

We knew we wanted each other in the way those
who become lovers do—with simultaneously a supernatural conviction of unexpressed mutual desire and a
mortal unsureness concerning declaration and consummation. The dilemma was magnified in this situa-
tion by the necessarily clandestine conditions of
our knowing and not knowing what we hoped and
feared for.

I accompanied Patrick when he officiated at services, and I walked around his parish with him, to
fetch the newspaper and on other daily errands. My
presence at his side brought blushes of hidden desire
and pleasurable jealousy to the cheeks of girls and
women we would meet. I realised that our emanation
of eros afforded collective release, whereas the knowledge that we were lovers would have provoked a
lynching. Not for the vow betrayed, but for the with-

drawing of his gift of sex—which was integral to the social efficacy of his priesthood—from all to one.

Patrick begged me to "take love easy as the leaves grow on the tree." But he also made himself clear: "No man, having put his hand to the plough, and looking back, is fit for the kingdom of God" (Luke 9:62). Between the carefree song of Yeats and this wages of sin verse, my penance of love was solemnised. Does it not always proceed so?

Love-making is never simply pleasure. Sex manuals or feminist tracts which imply the infinite plasticity of position and pleasure, which counsel assertiveness, whether in bed or out, are dangerously destructive of imagination, of erotic and of spiritual ingenuity. The sexual exchange will be as complicated as the relationship in general—even more so. Kiss, caress and penetration are the relation of the relation, body and soul in touch, two times two adds up: three times three is the equation. The three I harbour within me—body, soul and paraclete—press against the same triplicity in you. What I want, my overcharged imagination, released inside your body, taken up into mine, with attack and with abandon, succumbs so readily and with more joy than I could claim, to your passion, pudency and climax.

The Name: there is yet the Name. The Name of the Beloved cried out in rhythmic throes words the world: it abolishes the safe uncanniness of the ordinary, when the world is normally absent to the word. My name at every thrust returns me not to myself, but to the root of you flush in me.

Night time is psyche time: the accumulation of excess emotion, aroused but unattended during the day; it must have its say—in dream or in prayer, in love making and taking. Neglected or unrehearsed, these residues exact their revenge: they trouble my sleep or keep me awake with an acuity unknown to the day.

Morning is holy terror: awakening, a naked dawning with no consolation of the work of mourning. Grief has been expended during the night; curiosity for the day is still held at bay. There can be no preparation or protection for this moment of rootless exposure; the comforting contraries of diurnal acknowledgement are in suspense. Eros passion is fled: its twin, the passion of faith, is taunting my head.

To spend the whole night with someone is *agapē*: it is ethical. For you must move with him and with yourself from the arms of the one twin to the abyss of the other. This shared journey, unsure yet close, honesty embracing dishonesty, changes the relationship. It may not be a marriage, but it will be sacramental even without benefit of sacraments. To navigate this together is to achieve the mundane: to be present to each other, both at the point of difficult ecstasy and at the point of abyssal infinity, brings you into the shared cares of the finite world.

There are always auguries, not only of future difficulties but also of impossibility: these remain in negligible abeyance as long as both Lovers are in riskful engagement. How, you may ask, could I not have been aware of this impossibility as well as the difficulties inherent in this love affair? As my stepfather, who is unshockable, commented, when I related to him the outlines of my predicament, "You are having an affair with a married man," a bride of Christ, but also a vestal if not a virtual virgin. (Irving also ascertained that his fellow Irishman shared his fancy for the horses.) Yet even the details of this especially narratable story are quite generally transferable: someone who seems free may turn out to be encumbered.

I choose this particular story because it accentuates the predictable pattern: the Beloved is bereft of the Lover; she must become the Lover: she must generate love but without the love she received.

Why is it so agonising to the Beloved when the

Lover wards off love? The answer "loss" repeats the question. This conversion out of love, its incompletion, is the illimitable medium of this whole composition. It is the point at which lovelessness confesses that she is investigating herself. Can this be sound method? Sheridan said of Scholasticus that he wanted to learn to swim without entering the water. Here, the method must be circular, and that is why it is not vitiated. Well, I am immersed. But if I am floundering, can I be saved by thrashing around?

So what does bitter innocence claim? The Beloved says that she remains steadfast and consistent, unwavering in her love: the Lover is the inconsistent one. The Beloved says she is bewildered and deserted: the Lover appears indifferent equally to his withdrawal and to her bereavement. The Beloved remembers not only disproportionate joy, but the fantasy of the future pledged: "You are for me a vast, open space of unpressurised love." He covers his eyes with index finger and thumb: "I hate conversations like this."

Hands no longer marvel at the beauty of hands: they cease to stroke, slowly, repeatedly, the long, speechful fingers; her hands can no longer reach their short, maladroit, childlike friends. Palm no longer paddles in palm, kissing with inside lip.

Lips still meet lips, full enough for breach of promise, unlike the lipless organs of politicians. Lip no longer sucks in lip, tongue roving around the song-lines, greeting whorl upon whorl of inner ear. The embrace of face by face is the true carnival of sex beyond gender.

He no longer calls my name. (He no longer even uses my name.)

"Loss" is a loose description. The movement from eros passion through the passion of faith to the every-day and the ethical, enhanced when together and, equally, when apart, is missing. In place of the unself-consciousness of mutual love, its berth of listening stillness, a hateful self-regard is unleashed to gnaw the Beloved, the disappointed one.

Loss is legion. If the Lover finds the entangle-ment of love too harrowing, then, as it pulls back, his harrow crushes the Beloved, also caught in its path. Lover and Beloved are equally at the mercy of emo-tions which each fears will overwhelm and destroy their singularity. For the Lover, these are the frighten-ing feelings roused by the love: for the Beloved, these are the frightening feelings trusted to love, but now sent back against her. Patient, she is now doubly vio-lent agent: against his killed desire and against her desire returned. He covers his eyes with index finger and thumb and says, "This is not my story."

Let me then be destroyed. For that is the only way I may have a chance of surviving. Let those feelings uniquely called forth by sexual love, my life's passion and pain, my learnt desirability figured out of my primeval undesirability, let them prevail. Now I am not dissociated from my ululation. I hear the roaring and the roasting and know that it is I. Resist the telephone! Even though help is only a few digits away. For the first time, I say "No" to any alleviation, to the mean of friendship, to the endlessly inventive love of my sisters. I don't want to be justified. Keep your mind in hell and . . . I want to sob and sob and sob . . . until the prolonged skrieking bcomes a shout of joy.

"Loss" means that the original gift and salvation of love have been degraded: love's arrow poisoned and sent swiftly back into the heart. My time-worn remedy has been to pluck the arrow and to prove the wound, testing its resources with protestant concentration. This time I want to do it differently. You may be weaker than the whole world but you are always stronger than yourself. Let me send my power against my power. So what if I die. Let me discover what it is that I want and fear from love. Power and love, might and grace. That I may desire again. I would be the Lover, am barely the Beloved.

I have not yet told the whole of this story. This time, unhappy love, sempiternal, has an additional declension.

6

Suppose that I were now to reveal that
I have AIDS, full-blown AIDS, and have been
ill during most of the course of what I have
related. I would lose you. I would lose you to
knowledge, to fear and to metaphor. Such a
revelation would result in the sacrifice of the

alchemy of my art, of artistic "control" over the setting as well as the content of your imagination. A double sacrifice of my elocution: to the unspeakable (death) and to the overspoken (AIDS).

Not that I haven't been wooing you continually by the moods of metaphor; but we have kept the terms of our contract: you have given me free rein, and I have honoured my share of the obligation by not using up that freedom, by leaving large tracks of compacted equivocation at every twist in the telling.

Yet, do you not know and fear even more about love? Yes, yes, of course you do, but while the sorrows of love in their monotony are endlessly engaging, illness is intrinsically not. So why should I deliberately spoil this narration by reduced equivocation? I must continue to write for the same reason I am always compelled to write, in sickness and in health: for, otherwise, I die deadly, but this way, by this work, I may die forward into the intensified agon of living.

I do not have AIDS. Yet I seek to convey the impasses, the limitations and cruelties, equally, of alternative healing and of conventional medicine. I would insinuate *démarches* of healing that have not been imagined in either canon. I would oppose to the iatrogenic materiality of medicine and to the screwtape overdose of spirituality of alternative healing, *love's work*, the work I have been charting, accomplishing, but, above all and necessarily, failing in, all along the way.

If I were now to explain that, in my early forties, I have cancer, say, advanced ovarian cancer, which has failed to respond to chemotherapies, and is spread throughout the peritoneum, the serous membrane lining the cavity of the abdomen, and in the pleura, the serous lining of the lungs, you would respond according to the exigencies of taxonomy, symbol and terror, according to ignorance rather than knowledge, although there is, in fact and in spirit, no relevant knowledge. For you, "cancer" means, on the one hand, a lump, a species of discrete matter with multiplying properties, on the other hand, a judgement, a species of ineluctable condemnation.

To the bearer of this news, the term "cancer" means nothing: it has no meaning. It merges without remainder into the horizon within which the difficulties, the joys, the banalities, of each day elapse.

Dare I continue? Are you willing to suspend your prejudices and judgement? Are you willing to confront and essay a vitality that overflows the bumble mix of average well-being and ill-being—colds and coughs and flu, periodic lapses in the collaboration with culture, or headachy days, when one feels gratuitously lacking in inclination, never mind inspiration? For what people now seem to find most daunting with me, I discover, is not my illness or possible death, but my accentuated being; not my morbidity, but my renewed vitality. He covers his eyes with index finger and thumb and says *to me*, "I feel old and tired and sick."

With a man in clerical orders, one may legitimately expect him to have faced eternity. The source of his authority will be this humility in relation to his own mortality. It should seal him from violence in love, from joining the hierarchies of exterminating angels. With a consultant surgeon, alas, you cannot expect him necessarily to have faced his own finality. Surgeons are not qualified for the one thing with which they deal: life. For they do not understand, as part of their profession, "death," in the non-medical sense, nor therefore "life" in the meaningful sense, inclusive of death. When they fail to "cure," according to their own lights, they deal out death: "You won't die at eighty of boredom." "Since you may well die within a year of your operation, it is not worth spoiling your remaining time with more chemotherapy that will make you deaf."

Mr Wong always puts all the lights on immediately, even before he enters your room. Whether he
is coming to chat or to examine you, before his
requirements or yours have been exchanged, regardless of whether you have visitors or are alone, whatever you are doing—reading, watching television,
thinking quietly in the twilight—Mr Wong snaps on
the lights. The Englishman's Englishman, he is short
and wears a smart, mottled suit and colourful bow-tie.
He regales you, with wide, unblinking eyes, for half an
hour with the tale of his surgical exploits that day, in
the days to come, in days or years past. When you
express the admiration called for by the recitation of
the drama of his endless vocation, he dismisses your
gestures with histrionic largesse.

Mr Wong is the best of his kind: he is a truly bril-
liant surgeon. He relishes the difficult case, when he
must exercise quick judgement and manual dexterity
in the face of the unexpected. Mr Wong rightly de-
serves the esteem of his colleagues, his patients and,
most significantly, the nurses, who are unanimous
that, if the circumstances arose, they would want to be
treated by him.

Nurses belong to the lowest hierarchy of exterminating angels: principalities, archangels and angels.

To their bastion of superfemale skill, their power and love, may be attributed the protection of the surgeons from the crisis of authority that otherwise troubles modernity. Only the Bishop of Coventry, my bemused, stumbling friend, who came to help me push gently forward, had more inviolable authority bestowed by the nurses on to him and his pathetic posy of fragrant garden flowers, which nestled humbly among the hosts of assertive bouquets.

"Nurse is coming," croons the loudspeaker system, on the patient's request for assistance. A multiple female beast, with millions of eyes and heads and breasts and arms and good intentions, is invoked by this collective noun. "Nurse," who invariably enters without putting on the lights, is a supernatural being. She executes endless good works, and she offers her soul as well as her skill. She, too, has turned anguish into care; but she has not been spoilt by status into imagining that she decrees destiny. Unfortunately, she believes that the surgeon does; her natural scepticism somehow changed by her training into unassailable fundamentalism.

The nursing body defies not only the crisis of authority but also the crisis of gender. I met only one male nurse among what must be about fifty meetings with individual nurses, whose names I always request and learn immediately so that we may also exist for each other as single beings as well as impersonal functions. The nursing hierarchies are sororities, where women order, and co-operate with and cherish each other, under ultimate circumstances, with strictly limited power. The Cancer Ward, after the vow is taken, becomes the unconscious horizon for the normal range of nursing nuance and action. Once in uniform and in role, these women assume a femininity which leaves no opportunity for manoeuvre; *a fortiori*, none for subversion.

On my last day at the hospital, after my first operation (a total hysterectomy, removal of the caecum (appendix), omentum and 20 per cent of the large bowel, closed with a temporary colostomy), I asked Mr Wong, "What makes a man become a gynaecologist?" He replied, "Some men love women, and some men hate women"—no admission of unresolved equivocation in that taut response. And what makes a man become a specialist in gynaecological cancer (a field "invented" in the last twenty years)? He will always be breaking the bad news to individual women concerning their female anatomy. And what makes a man a specialist and co-author of the latest, standard

textbook on ovarian cancer? Mr Wong answers prag-
matically, "I was good with my hands but didn't want
to become an obstetrician like my father."

I am well placed to understand this combative
emulation of the immediate ancestor. Is it not said,
"Don't shave your beard, and then your son will shave
his"? This tradition is only just beginning to acknowledge that its women tell tales, too. "Paint your nails
and lips, wear jewellery, except on the Sabbath, and
then your daughter will desist from adornment but
keep the faith." These monitory anecdotes indicate,
however, the anxiety of modernity.

What kind of faith can a man have, who special-
ises in cancer? "Agnosticism," emphasises Mr Wong. "I
know there is no natural justice, because you, who
have harmed no one, have cancer, while Saddam
Hussein does not. I don't know any more if there is
divine justice."

The "silent" cancer: 80 per cent are discovered in
an advanced state with widespread metastases. "Silent,"
too, in the public debate over universal screening for
breast cancer and regular cervical smears. I had a
smear and internal examination in February; at the
end of March, the same doctor discovered a swelling,
"the size of a melon," whether attached to womb or

ovaries, one or both, he did not know. "Fibroid uterus," he diagnosed. The consultant in the local hospital said a few days later, "There is a distinct possibility that it is cancer." When I riposted jauntily and with earnest pathos, "I am the happiest, healthiest person I know," his grey eyes looked straight at me: "Well, you are going to be very severely tried." I like him for putting it like that. It leaves me be.

I could compose a divan of divination, an anthology of aetiologies:

Camille Paglia (American author and media personality): "Nature's revenge on the ambitious, childless woman."

Braham Murray (theatre director, my first cousin): "Your inspiration poisoned at source."

John Petty (Provost of Coventry Cathedral and faith healer): "Transgenerational haunting and possession."

Ian Florian (Principal, College of Traditional Acupuncture): "Imbalance of energies necessary for a woman to sustain success in the world."

Your betrayal twice by family; ancient, unacknowledged and unmourned dead; the philosophy of Hegel and Adorno; recent bereavements; the wrong kinds of relationship with men; too much whiskification; too little red wine and garlic. Hold on, I take garlic in my coffee . . . Well!

The "cancer personality," described by the junk literature of cancer, covers everyone and no one. Characteristics: obesity, anorexia, depression, elation (manic depression), lack of confidence, no satisfying or challenging work, poor relationships. The case histories sketch no-hopers, saved by cancer. Cancer gives them their last and first opportunity to admit and explore deep unhappiness and chronically unhealthy lifestyles. So eager are the authors to prove that no one is beyond hope that they select and focus on damaged and abject personalities. This produces the opposite of their intention. On the one hand, it can describe anyone and so fails to isolate a specific "cancer personality." On the other hand, the personalities are so utterly miserable, it provides no incentive for identifying one's own mix of blessings and curses.

It seems that my very fitness and agility, mental and physical, led me to overlook my condition. I am so attuned to regular exercise of body and mind that I could easily take minor symptoms of ill-health in my stride. Two bouts of nausea after evenings of mild excess in six months were cured by a scant morning in bed; some untimely, intermittent sensations of pre-menstrual tension were put down hazily to signs of an early menopause. I was cycling to and from the swimming pool five mornings a week and swimming my regular kilometre effortlessly, as I have done for the last ten years, up to the day before the first operation. My colleagues and friends and family are far more frail than I, with their colds and flu, bronchitis and allergies. Nor does this mean that I have not given frailty its due.

The consultant oncologist speaks in slow, measured tones in which her thoughtful mediation of the scientific framework to the kind of person she has in front of her is palpable. The alternate courses of carboplatin and cisplatin, first-line chemotherapy in ovarian cancer, are successful in "70 per cent" of cases. Their administration does not result in hair loss, and the nausea is controlled by the anti-emetic ondansetron. Nevertheless, she told me, "I am confident that the chemotherapy will be successful in the first instance."

Dr Jennifer Lord, with her long, straight black hair, smoothed to her head and neck, and her large, steady blue eyes, bears around her person *gravitas*, pace and concentration, qualities in short supply amidst the overcrowding and poor conditions of the Dudley Road Hospital, Dudley Road, Birmingham. The Dudley Road outside is almost impassable, like certain precincts of American cities. Poverty from every decade of the century seems to have been dumped here: boarded-up shops, wholesalers, the unemployed, countless furniture shops selling gaudy sofas too hard to sit on, five female dummies with kohl eyes in cheap saris, dishevelled children out of school. Huge advertisement hoardings sail majestically through the filthy screeching air, mocking the residents with their immaculate blandishments. We walked up and down the Dudley Road, hand in hand, waiting for the result of my blood test. Steve, who frequently accompanied me, found a workers' café, with dirty walls, chipped crockery and an old black-and-white telly, where we could get mugs of strong tea and look in a desultory way at a discarded *Sun*.

In the amorphous reception area of the hospital, large oblong notices in five oriental languages are perched above the lintels of the lifts to the right of the main entrance of the hospital and over the entrance to the main interior corridor, the longest hospital corridor in Europe. The English version declares: "If you feel you have waited an unduly long time, please contact the ambulance clerk or the receptionist." The people milling here cover the spectrum of the life-cycle: they look like "Mussulmen," the working prisoners of labour and death camps who give up the will to live, and lose the fierce, burning glare of starvation in their eyes. Hordes of people sitting in rows are condemned by those notices to the indifference marked by their contrary signification. All access and egress lies through this dispiriting terrace of deprivation.

St Chad, whose relics are enshrined in the Catholic Cathedral of Birmingham, was one of the most popular of medieval English saints. The eponymous chemotherapy unit, founded by Mr Wong, was translated to the Dudley Road Hospital when St Chad's Hospital was closed. The unit is carpeted in grey, and it is impressed upon the inmates that its appointment is far superior to other wards in the hospital. The conditions of treatment are unintentionally vicious. You must wait for a blood test, and nothing can happen until the results of the test are known. The nurse who takes blood is closed and ill-tempered. She treats you without grace in the corridor or in a public space within the unit, where people are slumped listlessly for hours. There is no privacy and there are no priorities. I stood up and kept urging that each consecutive stage of the treatment be carried out with alacrity. Normally needing no more than a book and a pitch of ground in which to sit splayed, with my knees bent back, so that my feet are at right angles to my thighs, I found that I needed to import company. To relieve the tedium and the tension of waiting, against the hosts of maundering television sets, I needed to hold on to a friend during the inevitable cannulation, the often clumsy and always painful insertion of the thin tube into a vein in the arm or wrist for the noxious, ultimate allopathy.

I went through this for the whole summer, every ten days; all, it transpired, to no avail. My well-differentiated cancer is chemotherapy-resistant.

In early September, I was unexpectedly released from the last three courses of chemotherapy, because I developed tinnitus, incessant ringing in the ears, and loss of high-tone hearing. It was the chubby-cheeked, jejune Senior Registrar who, in Dr Lord's unfortunate absence, insisted that, as my treatment was sheerly palliative, my life expectancy a year from the operation, I should not run the risk of further impairment to my hearing. Now, the consultants had conveyed to me that the aim was cure not palliation. With constant smiles, this "patient choice" was aimed straight at my heart. It

degraded the treatment; it debased my medical expec-
tations; it disdained my generally hopeful and trusting
outlook. When she returned, Dr Lord was laconic and
legitimate, as I knew she would be. "You will have
gained all the benefit you need. You may consider that
the treatment is finished."

The mid-September week in Wales with three
friends, to celebrate the end of the treatment prior to
the second operation to reverse the colostomy, proved
a cornucopia of delusive premonitions. Daily walks
lasting three to four hours unravelled the drama of
Pembrokeshire's prehistoric coastline. With seal col-
onies for kings, theriomorphic dominions in dizzying
ravines and hidden coves are inaccessible to the ultimate predators, but not to their sentimental, binocular
vision. An improvised whisky flask and a few bananas
provided our only sustenance. I kept easily apace with
my companions and was certain that there was no disease in my body.

This time of greatest intimacy between Steve and
me was also to be the last. In the half-week that he and
I spent together after our two friends had left, he
seemed marooned in a stilted affection, light-hearted
and adventurous, and then discomfited, as if he were

undergoing some esoteric ordeal of fellowship in which he was the initiate, I, the cypher.

Robert Jan van Pelt, Holocaust scholar extraordinaire, has examined 300 bundles of architectural plans, previously unopened since the war, in the archives of the museum at Auschwitz. These plans show Auschwitz to have been at the hub of the Nazi ambition to Germanise central Poland, a new installment of the medieval German tradition of colonisation of the East. The even tone of van Pelt's Dutch-accented Canadian voice becomes increasingly macabre as he shows slides from the archive: drawings of German trees to repopulate Polish forests, designs for German armchairs for off-duty SS officers, vernacular dog kennels for German hounds. Van Pelt argues that Auschwitz was first and foremost *a labour camp*: death was a by-product of the inclusion of individuals unsuited for work among the transports of potential workers—the displaced because displaceable Jews of Poland and Europe. On this account, the *Realpolitik* of land-hunger and labour is the motor of racism and genocide. Van Pelt is keen, moreover, to emphasise the contingent nature of many of the features of the so-called "Holocaust," which our use of holistic periphrasis tends to represent as predetermined and overly rational: the infamous barbed wire at the perimeter of the camp was initially stolen not supplied; the men's and women's barracks at Birkenau were designed with lack of foresight regarding the organisation of sanitation, and this resulted in much *unplanned* death.

The novelty of items that van Pelt wants to raise in the international debate means that, inadvertently but predictably, he is caught in the tightening coils of Holocaust ethnography, the typically meaningful orientation of current social and political action as constituting "the Holocaust," or folklore, if you like, as making its meaning. Caught, above all, concerning the practicalities of excrement, or, as he tersely puts it, concerning the subject of shit. People, he reports, are relatively inured to discussions of the design of gas chambers and inefficiency in the operation of the four crematoria. Yet, throughout Europe and North America, when he raises issues relating to the mismanagement of sanitation at the camps, he is met with reluctance, embarrassment and loss of attention.

Nowhere in the endless romance of world literature (my experience is, needless to say, limited) have I
come across an account of living with a colostomy.
Since the first colostomy was performed in this country in 1797, the first paper on the subject published in
1805, and colostomies have been routine medical
practice since the second half of the nineteenth century, this is more than enough time for lyric and
lament.

A colostomy is an opening of the colon on to the
abdomen: it is usually performed for people who have
had chronic bowel disorders. For them it is a great
relief, a new lease on life. I have no history of bowel
disorder. The remaining "seedlings," tiny pinpricks of
cancer, were located in the lining of the bowel, so that,
when 20 per cent of it was removed, together with the
other organs infected with metastases, the bowel was
not rejoined in case there might be growth of tumour
at the join. Leakage of bowel contents into the abdominal cavity is fatal. In principle, the colostomy was
temporary, to be reversed after the successful appli-
cation of chemotherapy, which would dissolve the
"seedlings."

Let me make myself clear: the colostomy—*stoma*
means "opening"—is a surrogate rectum and anus.

Tight coils of concentric, fresh, blood-red flesh, 25 millimetres (one inch) in diameter, protrude a few millimetres from the centre left of my abdomen, just below the waist. Blueness would be a symptom of distress.

This is comparatively easy to put into prose, because it is likely to be utterly unfamiliar. But how to inscribe my relation to its operation? "Changed body image" has already become an overworked cliché, which, anyhow, relates to motor and imaginary self-representation, and not to the re-siting of bodily function.

I want to talk about shit—the hourly transfiguration of our lovely eating of the sun. I need to remove the discourse of shit from transgression, sexual fetishism, from too much interest, but, equally, from coyness, distaste and the medical textbook. My interest is in the uncharted; my difficulty that I will inevitably enlist, by connotation and implication, the power and grace of the symbol. I need to invent colostomy ethnography.

What having a colostomy makes you realise is that normally you bear hardly any relation to your excrement. It is expelled from the body from an invisible posterior organ, and, with its characteristic solidity and odour, descends rapidly into water and oblivion. It is the sphincter muscle which affords the self-relation of retention and release. To exchange this discretion for an anterior cloaca and incontinence . . . how easy it is to borrow the prepared associations (Lou Andreas-Salomé famously pronounced that the vagina and rectum form one undifferentiated cloaca).

Deep brown, burnished shit is extruded from the bright, proud infoliation in a steady paste-like stream in front of you: uniform, sweet-smelling fruit of the body, fertile medium, not negative substance. It hangs hot in a bag, flush with the abdomen, with the raised temperature even of congealed life. This is to describe a new bodily function, not to redescribe the old. The organ of this facture has achieved that pipe-dream of humanity: evacuation of the body is far removed from the pudenda, pleasure and pain. There are no nerve-endings and there is no sensation in the stoma.

I am frequently asked whether I nourish the rancorous sentiment "Why me?" The unemphatic truth is that I have trouble imagining, publicly or privately, that everyone is not made exactly as I am myself. Suppose beings which solely urinate were all changed to beings which also defecate? This collective transition would be in effect no change at all. Suppose we all awoke one day with four faces, each one going straight forward: whither the spirit was to go, they go; and they turn not when they go. It makes all the difference: it makes no difference at all. It becomes routine; my routine is unselfconscious about the rituals and private character of your routines. Thus, I handle my shit. I no longer employ the word as an expletive, discharging intense, momentary irritation into its void of meaning.

The recovery of memory after an anaesthetic can be discontinuous: you may recover enough for communication, and then lapse into unconsciousness again. When you eventually emerge into continuous consciousness, you may have lost the knowledge imparted to you in the intermittent state. I asked Mr Wong to put a piece of paper in my hands with the news of the success of the second operation written on it, so that I could avoid the experience after the first operation of waking up in great pain in windowless, subterranean intensive care, not knowing whether the operation had taken place, although I had registered that knowledge in the recovery room. This time, I reasoned, I could bear the pain from the laparotomy more easily if I knew that the operation had taken place.

When I opened my eyes, I held in my hand a small piece of paper on which was written in block capitals: I AM VERY SORRY BUT WE WERE UNABLE TO REMOVE THE COLOSTOMY. And now the carnival of communication commenced.

Mr Wong came to see me soon after I regained consciousness. He was brisk and business-like. I had instructed him before the operation to relay its results solely to me, and not to my family, aware that a margin of interpretation was probable. The perceived effects of the chemotherapy could have ranged from complete elimination of the "seedlings" through any percentage of partial elimination. The worst outcome would be if the disease had "progressed." I wanted control over the broadcasting of any ambiguities.

"Control" in this context has two distinct meanings, both equally crucial. In the first place, "control," as you would expect, means priority and ability to manage, not to force, the compliance of others, to determine what others think or do. In the second, more elusive sense—a sense which, nevertheless, saves my life and which, once achieved, may induce the relinquishing of "control" in the first sense—"control" means that when something untoward happens, some trauma or damage, whether inflicted by the commissions or omissions of others, or some cosmic force, one makes the initially unwelcome event one's own inner occupation. You work to adopt the most loveless, forlorn, aggressive child as your own, and do not leave her to develop into an even more vengeful monster, who constantly wishes you ill. In ill-health as in unhappy love, this is the hardest work: it requires taking in before letting be.

Mr Wong did not waste a word, and for that I was grateful. He informed me that there was considerable progression of the disease. The "seedlings," pin-pricks just visible to the naked eye, had grown to a centimetre and spread further in the bowel lining, so that there was no healthy bowel to rejoin to healthy bowel. In addition, a thin, flat cake of tumour, 15 centimetres (6 inchs) in diameter, was attached to the greater curvature of the stomach and the old wound. When I asked Mr Wong why he had not removed this, he explained that removal would risk perforation of the small bowel, the rejoining of which would not necessarily endure, with risk of leakage, or it could develop into a fistula, which would digest the abdominal wall. Mr Wong said that there was so much cancer in me that it was not worth while selecting any part for surgical removal. He explained that I would have "second-line" chemotherapy. Meanwhile, his prognosis, he declared, was "guarded."

I was so overwhelmed by all this *unequivocal* information that any disappointment at the non-reversal of the colostomy receded far behind the new horizon. Before the operation, Mr Wong had appraised my general well-being, but he had not examined me. He had assured me that the chance of failure was "remote."

Enter Mr Bates. Mr Bates is the bowel specialist who operates with Mr Wong in cases of ovarian cancer, the pattern of whose metastases typically involves the bowel. A former Rhodesian, Mr Bates is large, alternately bluff and jovial; he belongs to a Scottish malt whisky fraternity. I first met him when I found myself in intensive care after the first operation. An unknown man, dressed in brightly coloured sports clothes (it was a Sunday), was bouncing up and down beside my cot. He enquired breezily, "How are you, young lady?" Through the haze of pain, I replied with outrage, "How dare you call me 'young lady,'" and demanded that the intruder introduce himself. This act of gross impropriety on my part in the mode of address, or rather, return of address, to a very senior consultant surgeon, who, moreover, like Mr Wong and the anaesthetist, was treating me gratis in a private hospital, enhanced my kudos in Mr Wong's eyes, and he took every opportunity to remind me of this picaresque solecism. Mr Bates and I became wary sparring partners. I always greeted him with the appellation "Young Man," and I presented him with unwanted volumes of Marx so that he might correct the vulgarity of his right-wing misapprehensions of the socialist theory of politics and society.

Mr Bates's visits were rare, a couple of times a week, whereas Mr Wong came to see me twice a day, regularly. Mr Bates was unperturbed, dispelling the tense aura prevailing in my room: "You look just the same inside as you did when we closed you up in April. No less cancer but no more either." "What about the flat cake of tumour?" I asked, amazed. "That's just adhesion of old scar tissue to the wound." Then he said a beautiful thing: "You are living in symbiosis with the disease. Go away and continue to do so."

Later that evening, I asked Dr Lord, who had arrived to discuss further treatment with me, whether she could advise me on how to reconcile, without offence, these utterly discrepant opinions, delivered by the two surgeons who had twice operated on me together. By now, too, I had been back under general anaesthetic at ten minutes' notice, because the suturing was not holding and the wound was gaping and pouring blood. It was an emergency: the fresh stitching more difficult than anticipated because of the prevalence of tumour. Yet even this unexpected opportunity for inspection produced no clarification. I emerged from the anaesthetic screaming with physical and mental distress. Even the highest dose of morphine did not relieve the tightness of the stitches. And Steve, whose resplendent aesthetic of bright yellow wool jacket had accompanied my anaesthetised eyes, Steve had not waited for me to return from the theatre.

Dr Lord left the room. In a few minutes she returned with Mr Wong. Then bedlam broke loose: "I will not talk to my colleague. I will not change my position. This is my cancer." In the ensuing ten minutes I summoned all the resources at my panicked disposal. I pleaded, cajoled, begged, flattered, inveigled Mr Wong to talk to his colleague, Mr Bates. I argued that my respect for my consultants was such that I could not proceed unless I understood the relation between their different views of my condition.

It was not in my interest that those conflicting judgements should be compromised: my light lies in their discrepancy. Mr Wong returned twenty-four hours later, having spoken to Mr Bates, with the composite proposition, "There is some progression, but it is minimal." By then, I was already in a realm beyond medicine. Dr Lord had added her hunch to the mêlée. She advised me against further chemotherapy at present, given the vigour of my current good health. With her customary care and caution, Dr Lord ventured the prediction that I might enjoy "many months" of further good health. Her principle that quality of life is as critical as life itself was clearly the basis of this deduction. I only had ears, however, for the counterfactuals in her ostensibly encouraging words: that, potentially, I have less than months of well-being, and, eminently, not years.

This sentencing, too, accelerated my release and departure from the distintegrating authority of conventional medicine. Medicine and I have dismissed each other. We do not have enough command of each other's language for the exchange to be fruitful. It is as if, exiled for ever into a foreign tongue, you learn the language by picking up words and phrases, even sentences, but never proceed to grasp the underlying principles of grammar and syntax, which would give you the freedom to use the language creatively and critically. You cannot generate the grammar of judgements in order to pursue alternative questions and conclusions. This, of course, assumes that there is a grammar at stake, and not simply a pragmatics, presented with the spurious legitimacy of a structure. I perceive all the more pellucidly the subliminal beat: what you cannot cure, you condemn, so that you restore the equilibrium of your dangerous inner impulses.

If I am mute, then so is medicine. It can no more fathom my holistic and spiritual matrix than I can master its material syntax. I must return to my life affair. It was never, of course, in abeyance: while I was in the theatre, it was waiting impatiently in the coulisses to reclaim its dancing partner for the never-ending Bacchanalian revel in which no member is not drunk, yet because each member collapses as soon as he drops out, the revel is just as much transparent and simple repose.

The resumption of the revel did not turn out to be straightforward. For if I had escaped with resolution one hierarchy of exterminating angels, I was immediately confronted with the rigid, smiling faces of yet another celestial hierarchy. From the iatrogenic materiality of medicine to the screwtape spirituality of alternative healing, I am prescribed these equally sickly remedies in a combined dosage which characterises the postmodern condition itself. My friends and family field the crisis of their own mortality brought on by my illness by serving hard and fast at me the literature and liquids of alternative healing.

If I have understood the limitations of my speaking in the esoteric but fatal language of clinical control, it is far more difficult to articulate the deadly blandishments of the exoteric language of cosmic love. This language propagates the paradox and pathos of the lonely-hearts column in the *New York Review of Books*. Literati describe themselves with the same cultured and idealising fantasy that has led them, after decades of semi-experience limited by just that fantasy, to the desperation of self-advertisement in those august columns. O violence in love!

The injunction, which pervades the literature of alternative healing, to become "exceptional" (Bernie Siegal), or "edgeless" (Stephen Levine), to assume unconditional love, is poor psychology, worse theology and no notion of justice at all. While presenting itself as a post-Judaic, New Age Buddhism, this spirituality re-insinuates the most remorseless protestantism. It burdens the individual soul with an inner predestination: you have eternal life only if you dissolve the difficulty of living, of love, of self and other, of the other in the self, if you are translucid, without inner or outer boundaries. If you lead a normally unhappy life, you are predestined to eternal damnation, you will not live.

This is the counsel of despair which would keep the mind out of hell. The tradition is far kinder in its understanding that to live, to love, is to be failed, to forgive, to have failed, to be forgiven, for ever and ever. Keep your mind in hell, and despair not.

A crisis of illness, bereavement, separation, natural disaster, could be the opportunity to make contact with deeper levels of the terrors of the soul, to loose and to bind, to bind and to loose. A soul which is not bound is as mad as one with cemented boundaries. To grow in love-ability is to accept the boundaries of oneself and others, while remaining vulnerable, woundable, around the bounds. Acknowledgement of conditionality is the only unconditionality of human love.

Exceptional, edgeless love effaces the risk of relation: that mix of exposure and reserve, of revelation and reticence. It commands the complete unveiling of the eyes, the transparency of the body. It denies that there is no love without power; that we are at the mercy of others and that we have others in our mercy. Existence is robbed of its weight, its gravity, when it is deprived of its agon. Instead of insinuating that illness may better prepare you for the earthly impossibilities, these enchiridions on Faith, Hope and Love would condemn you to seek blissful, deathless, cosmic emptiness—the repose without the revel.

I reach for my favourite whisky bottle and instruct my valetudinarian well-wishers to imbibe the shark's oil and aloe vera themselves. If I am to stay alive, I am bound to continue to get love wrong, all the time, but not to cease wooing, for that is my life affair, *love's work*.

7

Shortly after his mother died, when he was already ill himself, Jim sent me the following poem by Pier Paolo Pasolini, in a letter, which contained no comment on it:

GILLIAN ROSE

Prayer to My Mother

It's so hard to say in a son's words
what I'm so little like in my heart.

Only you in all the world know what my
heart always held, before any other love.

So, I must tell you something terrible to know:
From within your kindness my anguish grew.

You're irreplaceable. And because you are,
the life you gave me is condemned to loneliness

And I don't want to be alone. I have an infinite
hunger for love, love of bodies without souls.

For the soul is inside you, it is you, but
you're my mother and your love's my slavery:

My childhood I lived a slave to this lofty
incurable sense of an immense obligation.

It was the only way to feel life,
the unique form, sole colour; now it's over.

We survive in the confusion
   of a life reborn outside reason.

I pray you, oh I pray: Don't die.
I'm here, alone, with you in a future April ...

Sending me this poem was the prelude to a series of confessional letters, in which Jim put his self-alienation into world literature at the service of the examination of his life—the life of a philosopher, musician and aesthete, "a dandy of thought," as he referred wryly to himself.

I first met Jim in New York in August 1970. I had been in New York for three days. He invited me to go to a concert with him in Central Park to hear Alicia de Larrocha play Liszt and Ravel. It was a dramatic pause in my first few days of furious tourism.

The skyscrapers of the city rise in mammoth ter-races all around the steaming, wide open ground. The tiny hand-span of the lady playing the grand piano in the park belies the immensity of the sound which, beyond nature and *technē*, soars into the empyrean. In the intervals, Jim tells me about his work on Nietzsche's *The Birth of Tragedy out of the Spirit of Music*. I feel the stirrings again of my original passion for philosophy, which three years at Oxford have almost completely expunged. Instead of staying in New York for the three weeks planned, I decide to stay for a year.

It was my *Lehrjahr*, my real apprenticeship, after the *borniert* complacencies of my undergraduate education. What did I discover in that year? Jim, continental philosophy (Kant, Hegel, Nietzsche, Husserl, Heidegger), the Second Vienna School (Schoenberg, Webern, Berg), Abstract Expressionism (Clyfford Still, Mark Rothko, Barnett Newman, Morris Louis), cooking (out of Craig Claiborne and Alice B. Toklas), hashish, LSD, popular music (Grateful Dead, Bob Dylan, Rolling Stones—yes, in New York!), homosexuality, Jim, Häagen-Dazs ice-cream, the German language, Harlem (where I taught black teenage delinquents to read, two afternoons a week), Adorno, Jim.

Everything about Jim was in huge proportions: over six foot three, he was lean and lanky, with a luxuriant mantle of shining jet hair cast carelessly over his elongated back, and a leopard walk, his limbs curving forward like a giant, caged cat. Jim had the most majestic hands; to say they were the hands of a keyboard player would understate their magnitude and grace. They were hands from the workshop of Henry Moore, with immense, broad, flat fingers, languid under their intelligent weight. At the piano, these organs were possessed, animated by the contortions of Scriabin's music, in the disciplined expression of an emotional range which no other medium afforded him.

Not philosophy, and this was Jim's tragedy. He found no way—not even Nietzsche's example—of bringing his inner emotional turmoil into his philosophy, his discipline, his art. Philosophy remained cleverness, a game, but not a stage on life's way; it remained *aesthetic without an oeuvre*, as did everything and everyone else for him.

It was other gay friends of Jim's who told me much later that Jim had been an *habitué* of the New York Baths. I was shocked, not out of naivety or prudery concerning the culture of the baths, but out of surprise at what this participation implied about Jim's degree of sexual energy. When I had once made some offhand remark about his erotically cultivated dress and gait, but his low vitality and disinclination for the act, he had reassured me, "Don't worry, my male lovers complain, too."

After a period during which he taught philosophy at Bennington College, Vermont, one of the very few schools in the States which would employ someone without a PhD, Jim returned to New York. He had been asked to leave Bennington on the charge of corruption of students. As with Socrates, Jim's students were his art: he was an inspired teacher, whose classes and more casual imparting of his vast knowledge and deep understanding of philosophy and music would provide a lifelong impulsion in the intelligent young.

In New York, Jim returned to a tiny apartment at Broadway and 111th Street, sucking on the south breast of Columbia University, with the intricate façade of the Cathedral of St John the Divine abutting on the east end of the street. He was to stay in this apartment until he lay dying on the filthy mattress on the floor. The two dark, airless rooms, joined by a narrow corridor with a cooking alcove and bathroom, contained all his belongings, including an upright piano, which had overflowed much more spacious abodes.

Jim included the following passage from *The Wicked Pavilion* (1954) by Dawn Powell in one of his letters to me:

Sloane, so it seemed to him now, had never had to make a decision before in his life. There were always two paths, and if you stood long enough at the crossroads, one of them proved impassable. There were always two women, but one of them wouldn't have you or one of them kidnapped you. There were always two careers, but at the crucial moment one of them dropped out, something happened, somebody made an appointment, and there you were. For Dalzell Sloane, destiny had shaped itself only through his hesitation . . . There were people, and Dalzell was one of them, who were born café people, claustrophobes unable to endure a definite place or plan. The café was a sort of union station where they might loiter, missing trains and boats as they liked, postponing the final decision to go any place or do anything until there was no longer any need for decision. One came here because one couldn't decide where to dine, whom to telephone, what to do . . . One might be lonely, frustrated, or heartbroken, but at least one wasn't sewed up.

Jim met Camille when they were both teaching at Bennington. Camille was also asked to leave after she was involved in a fistfight at a college dance. Camille was also an outstanding teacher and fraternised with her adoring students. At Jim's hiring interview, the Principal of the College laconically described the student body as formed by "the cubs of our most successful predators." Corruption was not a hieratic privilege; it was the only demotic virtue of the

College. Once Jim and Camille arrived at a party in New York together, in drag: Jim, with clumsily applied eye make-up, Camille with her hoydenish cross-dressing.

Over the years, Jim and Camille appeared like a perennially happy and unhappy married couple. Emotionally dependent on each other, they would bicker and fight and compete in cunning vindictiveness; yet this was combined with genuine concern for each other. What they shared was a hyperactive erotic fantasy—one not necessarily reflected in their actual relationships—and an insatiable investment in the style of the aesthete. Intellectually, they diverged radically. Camille is a literary wordsmith, as voracious in her writing as in her reading. She is convinced of her originality and dismissed Jim's urgings that she read Lacan, to temper the archetypal pattern of *Sexual Personae*. Jim was one of the few people who knew that Camille was writing *Sexual Personae* during the fifteen years of its gestation. If Camille served as the *alazon*, the Imposter, who boasts of more than she knows, then Jim played the role of the *eiron*, the Ironical Jester, who feigns ignorance and who knows much more than he reveals. Camille was impervious to the subtleties of Jim's compassion for her and her work. On many occasions, these two Old Comedians lapsed into irritable depression as a result of the pigheadedness of their trouble and strife—as each construed the other.

$\mathcal{L}$ance's body was put in a refrigerator for the first few days at the city hospital where he died of AIDS. At that time the nursing staff abhorred AIDS patients, so that food and care were provided by his friends to the former drag queen, who, in his last days, still attempted to apply make-up over the Kaposi's sarcoma that ravaged his ballerina face. When it was finally established that no will existed, and that there was no one with legal claim to the body, it was removed and sent to Potter's Field. Potter's Field is Hart Island in Long Island Sound, belonging to New York State, where the unclaimed bodies of the murdered, the intestate, the unidentified and the unidentifiable, are buried. Jim told me that he was "bombed out" with grief when Lance died. He wept for two weeks after his death.

Lance was Jim's true love: a former street urchin, who took to the East Side at the age of eight, after he had seen his father shoot himself. When Jim met him, Lance was already enthroned as one of New York's most delectable drag queens. Jim showed me with immense pride the billowing folds of the black silk costume with thousands of sequined eyes that Lance had sewn, sequin by sequin. Lance lived in Jim's apartment for ten years, on and off, first as Jim's lover, and then as his fitful friend and baneful child. Jim cared for Lance, providing a framework for the intermittent pilgrim, while Lance, dispossessed and hungry for learning—languages, music, philosophy and literature—became Jim's last, beloved student. Once Lance developed full-blown AIDS, the end came in a matter of weeks, for he was an ethereal being, all arabesque and delicate, sliver moon.

After the Bennington fiasco, Jim gave up philosophy as a profession. For fifteen years he took the subway every weekday from the Upper West Side to Brooklyn, where he worked for the New York City Police Department. He was the Senior Commissioner on a permanent commission into corruption in the New York City Police. Jim's speciality was the investigation of cocaine dealing among the police force. For eighteen years, since his time at Bennington, Jim had been habitually snorting cocaine. This addiction intensified exponentially after Jim inherited his parents' wealth and became ill himself.

Doctors do not make home visits in the States: it is too dangerous. "He has AIDS, but he is dying of starvation, depression and drug addiction," Jim's doctor declared soberly to Andrew and me. We had managed to persuade Jim to travel downtown to see his doctor after days of resistance, and then after hours on the day. Jim refused to leave his cold bath, and was only moved by my developing a severe nose-bleed. Like the Annunciation in Bruges in which the Madonna has a nose-bleed—Mary's response to the change of pressure caused by the archangel Gabriel's horrifying news of her divine election—the high pressure of Jim's perversity provoked my wordless torrent of frustration.

Andrew, former Bennington student, Jim's Ariel, had been keeping Jim alive with delicacies gleaned from his work as a chef. When we returned with Jim to the apartment, we set about trying to introduce some order and cleanliness into Jim's affairs so that we might have a chance of providing home nursing for him. Jim insisted that he would die if he were ever made to move from his apartment.

I find it impossible not to see that apartment, which is branded into my mind, as the emblem of the postmodern city. With its garish half-light provided day and night by a green and yellow Tiffany lamp, it was the veritable philosopher's cave. Crammed with the phantasmagoria of Western culture, everything, by the time we got to it, was in a more or less advanced state of decreation. The most mighty art books, multi-volume sets of the major philosophers in the original languages, Greek, German and French, a unique music collection comprising thousands of records, tapes and CDs, hundreds of American paperbacks of literature and philosophy—all were scored with dirt, infested with cockroaches, stale with dust and debris.

Fading divas and female film stars canted in one oblique corner of the room, while strong male nudes were unrobed in the bathroom. Jim's cult of the body was his response to his own which, when infant and child, his mother could never touch. The filthy carpets were littered with the last half-year's opened and unopened mail. In the course of sorting through it to pay his outstanding bills and to work out how much of his legacy remained, we could trace the acceler-ated pattern of cocaine consumption: a thousand dollars withdrawn every week for the previous six months.

Even if you are holding his hand, you can never be sure in what spirit your friend has died. Jim spent his last hours in the triage ward of a city hospital for people without health insurance. His three closest friends by his side, I whispered to him, "You are surrounded by friends who love you." Speechless for days, shrunken and orange with death, his breathing shallow and laboured, he took hold of the bed sheet, saturated with bright hospital blue, in both of his unearthly hands, and pulled it right up over his face. He was beyond language, but not beyond the discomforts of love.

Jim was a passionate fan of Isaiah Berlin and of Michel Foucault, both of whom he had met personally on visits which they had made at various times to New York. He asked me to obtain a copy of Alexander Herzen's *My Past and Thoughts* for him, because Isaiah Berlin claims somewhere that it is one of the great works of Russian literature. I found an edition without difficulty in a New York bookstore. Jim devoured it eagerly. However, it was the opening passage which he said eased what he called his "problem of self-representation":

Who is entitled to write his reminiscences?

Everyone

Because no one is obliged to read them.

In order to write one's reminiscences it is not at all necessary to be a great man, nor a notorious criminal, nor a celebrated artist, nor a statesman——it is quite enough to be simply a human being, to have something to tell, and not merely the desire to tell it but at least have some little ability to do so.

Every life is interesting; if not the personality, then the environment, the country are interesting, the life itself is interesting. Man likes to enter into another existence, he likes to touch the subtlest fibres of another's heart, and to listen to its beating . . . he compares, he checks it by his own, he seeks for himself confirmation, sympathy, justification . . .

8

King Arthur explained his dream of Camelot to Guinevere, his beloved wife. He would end the feuds and warfare between the barons and knights, not by becoming a tyrant or despot, but by becoming a just king, who would maintain the rule of law. He would give straight judgements to foreigners and to his own people, so that they would prosper and enjoy peace, not war. They would have plentiful harvests, not famine or blight or plague, and the women would bear children. In answer to Guinevere's doubts about the likely stability of this new regime of peace, King Arthur proposed to enlist the participation of the knights. He built a Round Table, emblem of equality, and sent out criers for the best knights to join the debate.

Launcelot, afar in France, heard of this vision of Camelot, and, like other warriors and wise men, he was eager to join the fellowship of the Round Table. Launcelot hoped that the new kingdom would create the perfect realm, whereas King Arthur's aim was to guarantee a knowable and reliable law, which would serve the people and their customs as they were. Guinevere and the other knights warned Arthur that Launcelot cared more for ideals than for others. However, they were all convinced of Launcelot's human heart when, in a jousting tournament, he wept as he slew a knight. So Launcelot became a Knight of the Round Table.

Launcelot and Guinevere fall in love. For some time, everyone except the King knows of their illicit passion. When the King finds out about it too, should he continue to pretend not to know what has happened, so as to preserve the vision of Camelot? This would destroy the authority of the Round Table and the law. Should he banish Launcelot and condemn Guinevere to die, according to the law, which they have all sworn impartially to uphold? If he enforces the law, against his desire, he will lose his beloved wife, who has betrayed him, and his beloved friend, Launcelot. The King carries out the law: Launcelot is banished and Guinevere is condemned to death. Launcelot saves Guinevere, who enters a convent, and he wages war against Arthur. King Arthur wins the war, but he loses Guinevere, Launcelot and the vision of Camelot.

Whatever King Arthur chooses, whether to overlook the betrayal or to prosecute the crime, the choice is not the issue. For, one way or the other, the King must now be sad. Betrayed or avenged, sadness is the condition of the King. Whether action is taken in the spirit of the law, or whether its requirements are ignored, the law will rebound against his human weakness so as to disqualify itself. Either its authority will be eroded by the deliberate oversight of the King, or, if executed, it will be overthrown by Launcelot's revenge.

This medieval tale contains Merlin's wisdom about the rule of reason. It tells what happens when a sovereign people ("the King") without coercion decree a law for themselves. Their humanity is forgotten, and so will be the law. Sadness is the condition of the King. For he has to experience his power and his vulnerability, his love and his violence, within and without the law.

Philosophy, ancient and modern, is born out of this condition of sadness. Metaphysics, which, in Aristotle's technical terms, is concerned with the relation between the universal "nose" and the sheer snubness of a nose, which no term can capture, this remote-sounding metaphysics is the *perplexity*, the *aporia*, at how to find the path from the law of the concept to the peculiarity of each instance, from "the nose" to the snub. If metaphysics is the *aporia*, the perception of the difficulty of the law, the difficult way, then ethics is the development of it, the *diaporia*, being at a loss yet exploring various routes, different ways towards the good enough justice, which recognises the intrinsic and the contingent limitations in its exercise. Earthly, human sadness is the divine comedy—the ineluctable discrepancy between our worthy intentions and the ever-surprising outcome of our actions. This comic condition is *euporia*: the always missing, yet prodigiously imaginable, easy way.

Modern and postmodern philosophers continue the sceptical conceit according to which philosophers affect disaffection from philosophy. Traditionally, this is the way in which philosophy reclaims its originality. Postmodern philosophers are in deadly, unironic earnest. Philosophy, they claim, is revenge for the unbridgeable distance between thought or language and concrete being; metaphysics is spleen at the diversity and difference of beings; ethics is the violent domination of the troubling otherness of the other. Postmodern philosophers say that philosophy is founded on the totalitarian ideal of Camelot, whereas philosophy is born out of the sadness of the King, to whom it offers the consolation of reflection.

Previously, modern philosophical *irrationalism* was seen retrospectively by philosophers and historians as the source of the racist and totalitarian movements of the twentieth century. Now, philosophical reason itself is seen by postmodern philosophers as the general scourge of Western history. To reason's division of the real into the rational and the irrational is attributed the fatal Manichaeism and imperialism of the West.

This decision by the intellectuals that reason itself has ruined modern life, and should be dethroned and banned in the name of its silenced others, is comparable to the decision to stop small children, girls and boys, from playing with guns, pugnacious video games, or any violent toys. This brutally sincere, enlightened probity, which thinks it will stop war and aggression, in effect aggravates their propensity. This decision evinces loss of trust in the way that play (fairy stories, terrifying films) teaches the difference between fantasy and actuality. The child who is able to explore that border will feel safe in experiencing violent, inner, emotional conflict, and will acquire compassion for other people. The child who is locked away from aggressive experiment and play will be left terrified and paralysed by its emotions, unable to release or face them, for they may destroy the world and himself or herself. The censor aggravates the syndrome she seeks to alleviate; she seeks to rub out in others the border which has been effaced inside herself.

Philosophers who blame philosophy for the ills of

civilisation have themselves lost the ability to perceive the difference between thought and being, thought and action. It is they who expunge the difference between fantasy and actuality, between the megalomania projected on to reason and the irreverent forces which determine the outcome of actual conflicts. They have inflated the power of philosophical reason, conferring on it a supposititious dangerous potency. It is the philosophers, not reason, who thereby degrade the independence of political realities and contingencies. Terrified of their own inner insecurity at the border between rationality and conflict, between the new academic political protestantism and politics as the art of the possible, they proceed as if to terminate philosophy would be to dissolve the difficulty of acknowledging conflict and of staking oneself within it. To destroy philosophy, to abolish or to supersede critical, self-conscious reason, would leave us resourceless to know the difference between fantasy and actuality, to discern the distortion between ideas and their realisation. It would prevent the process of learning, the corrigibility of experience. This ill-will towards philosophy misunderstands the authority of reason, which is not the mirror of the dogma of superstition, but risk.

Reason, the critical criterion, is for ever without ground.

𝓜y passion for philosophy began when I was seventeen. I read Plato's *Republic* and Pascal's *Pensées*. This is the only thing I have for which I am grateful to the local grammar school, which was otherwise the seat of academic narrowness and obsessive social propriety. The grandiose headmistress was equally mocked by her pupils, her staff and her own unfortunate, apt name, Miss Bland. With rapt but sober elation, I devoured the *Republic* and the *Pensées*, quintessential ancient and modern works, foundation of political philosophy and existential theology. I never found philosophy abstract or abstruse. The dramatic unfolding of both of these works, the one, a dialogue, in which the assent of the partner is continuously wooed, the other addressed to the perplexed, solitary soul, were anagogic: invitations to undertake singular journeys, which deepened and did not seek to placate the burgeoning sadness of the teenage soul. Perplexed, aporetic, not dogmatic, they indicated the difficulty of the way, and the routes to be essayed. I never discovered in them any *euporia*, any easy way or solution, any monologic, imperialist metaphysics. Philosophy intimated the wager of wisdom——as collective endeavour and as solitary predicament. It redeemed the earnest stupidity of my schooling.

It did not prepare me for the deeper stupidity of reading philosophy at university. The oppressive opulence of Oxford was married to a vision of philosophy which would have induced in me a lifelong alienation from it, had I not already made the pact with my *daemon*. At St Hilda's College, reading Philosophy, Politics and Economics, I was taught philosophy by Jean Austin, the widow of the philosopher J. L. Austin. Jean Austin had published a paper on "The Meaning of Happiness," for which she was well qualified in her aura of tense dejection, chain-smoking with shaky hands, her nails stained orange with nicotine. A cramped, nervous figure, she received us in the spacious, slow sitting-room overlooking the river and the Botanical Gardens. "Remember, girls, all the philosophers you will read are much more intelligent than you are." The vacant, derogatory ethos of this initiation could not hide the contrary truth. Jean Austin did not think females could be trusted to read philosophy, to play the game. Hand-picked and super-intelligent, they would either find the rules of the game fatuous, or, *horribile dictu*, they might imagine that philosophy had some substance which exceeded the celebrated idea that certain kinds of proposition have illocutionary or perlocutionary force. "You do understand, philosophy has absolutely no use at all."

I was an especial offender. In an essay I coupled Hume, required reading, with Diderot, another of my schoolday passions. I was sent away, my person pronounced perverse, to rewrite the essay. When I returned two days later with a string of passages from Hume, I was commended: "That's the best essay on Hume I've ever had." I accepted Jean Austin's praise graciously: "If that's the best essay on Hume you've ever had, it is because Hume wrote it." It was Jean Floud at Nuffield College who, in my final year, saved me from this pernicious nonsense. She greeted me on our first meeting in her utilitarian rooms, "How I dislike teaching undergraduates from the women's colleges. They will have been taught so badly." I bloomed in this degradation, and knew that I had met a kindred spirit. Jean Floud introduced me to sociological theory. Thus I resumed passionate, holistic, critical reading and thinking, which revived my earlier commitment to justice and to speculation.

At the end of my second term at Oxford, I failed my preliminary examination in formal logic. Over-prepared, I had completed the course before I arrived at the promiscuous portals of the university. I found logic easy, like Latin. I had forgotten the technical moves by the time I came to the examination. This fail-ure had other causes.

My so-called "adult" life began with the repeti-tion of my childhood trauma: the marriage between my mother and stepfather blew up in my face. I arrived at university with my heart in four quarters. I was given a scholar's room: it had the dubious privilege of no central heating, unlike the commoners' rooms on the same corridor. Only the bed or the immediate vicinity of the gas fire, which induced progressive somnolence, were tolerably warm. The view from the small, high window was stirring and strange—of the river, Magdalen Bridge and Tower and the Botanical Gardens.

I was disorientated by the incongruity between this fairy-tale beauty and my inner misery. I was unable to get out of bed in the mornings. The vast, indiffer-ent, cultivated space, stretching down over St Hilda's polished lawns and away in the distance, above which ascended steeples, turrets and castellations—the chorus of bells heralds the hours—induced in me acute agoraphobia. This condition was to accompany me throughout my twenties. Agoraphobia involves a magnification of space, populated by myriad terrors. Benign sights and sounds acquire a sinister, echoic, persecutory air, mocking your inability to connect signification with the world of objects. "Agoraphobia" is usually defined as fear of wide open space, but the word, more closely observed, is specific. *Agora* means the market-place, the place of assembly; it implies public, articulate space, space full of interconnections, with which you cannot enter into exchange. You feel as if you are suspended on the sharp rim of the world, of its space and of its signification. Virginia Woolf thought that the birds were speaking Greek, I hear bird-song as grief. The happy cries of schoolchildren at play are uniformed in viciousness. To this day, the steady roar of a motorcycle along a straight road at night resurrects in me this amorphous panic of articulation. This particular trigger is one manifestation of agoraphobia which I am able to apprehend, but not to demystify. As a graduate student in Oxford, I lived above an ironmonger's shop on the Cowley Road. One day, the furniture dealer in the shop next door left his wife; he purchased in compensation a motor-

cycle for their sixteen-year-old son. All the neighbour-
ing shopkeepers predicted an accident. The boy was
killed within two months. A row ensued about who
should attend the funeral.

I found myself in my first term at Oxford with
no home to return to, and Oxford was no home. My
mother and then my stepfather attempted suicide, or,
rather, *advertised* suicide. For if you want to die, you
die; and if you want to harry and torment your children, you make sure that they know of your intentions, which then, thank God, you do not carry
through. I received farewell phone calls in the College.
And then I couldn't get out of bed, forgot about logic,
and began to look for somewhere to live during the
vacation, when all undergraduates were required to
vacate their rooms. I tried to go home for a few days.
My stepfather—my kind, equanimous, humorous
stepfather—flung contraceptive pills at his two eldest
daughters, and commanded us with sour logic not to
marry as our mother had done, without experience.
We had been brought up dedicated to the double standard of female virginity, and my first term at Oxford
had not shaken that resolve of chastity. I left home
again and returned to the freezing attic room on the
Iffley Road, where I had to clamber into the bath with

the top half of my body fully clothed. It made me sob, that steaming hot water in the ice-bucket of the bare bathroom.

$\mathscr{D}$ante's poem is called *The Divine Comedy*. Sacrilegious poet! He usurped the impassible sceptre of Godhead to assign his friend and foe to the eternal terraces of the *paradiso* and the *inferno*. Does not all writing, even if it aims at *Gelassenheit*—to let things be—arrogate such illegitimate authority?

Philosophy provides a humbler definition of comedy, which eludes the hubris of the medieval poet: "The comical as such implies an infinite light-heartedness and confidence felt by someone raised altogether above his own inner contradiction and not bitter or miserable in it at all; this is the bliss and ease of a man who, being sure of himself, can bear the frustrations of his aims and achievements." This is Hegel's version of the divine comedy. No human being possesses *sureness of self*: this can only mean being bounded and unbounded, selved and unselved, "sure" only of this untiring exercise. Then, this sureness of self, which is ready to be unsure, makes the laughter at the mismatch between aim and achievement comic, not cynical; holy, not demonic. This is not love of suffering, but the work, the power of love, which may curse, but abides. It is power to be able *to attend*, powerful or powerless; it is love to laugh bitterly, purgatively, purgatorially, and then to be quiet.

I find it baffling that philosophers are currently claiming that we have a choice between three alternatives: revealed religion, enlightenment rationalism and postmodern relativism. "Revealed religion" refers to faiths which base their claim to truth on divine intervention and sacred scripture; "enlightenment rationalism" means the modern authority of unaided human reason, the ability of humanity to achieve unlimited progress and perfection; "postmodern relativism" renounces the modern commitment to reason in view of its negative outcome—the destructive potentiality of science, the persistence of wars and holocausts. It proposes pluralism, localism and reservation as principles, when it has abandoned principles.

It is *the unrevealed religion* which troubles us more than any revealed religion: the *unrevealed* religion which has hold of us without any evidences, natural or supernatural, without any credos or dogmas, liturgies or services. It is the very religion that makes us protest, "But I have no religion," the very *protestantism* against modernity that fuels our inner self-relation. Yet this very protest founded modernity. This self-reliance leaves us at the mercy of our own mercilessness; it keeps us infinitely sentimental about ourselves, but methodically ruthless towards others; it breeds sureness of self, not ready to be unsure, with an unconscious conviction of eternal but untried election. *Quotidie morimur et tamem nos esse aeternos putamus* (We die every day and therefore we consider ourselves to be immortal). This *unrevealed* religion is the baroque excrescence of the Protestant ethic: hedonist, not ascetic, voluptuous, not austere, embellished, not plain, it devotes us to our own individual, inner-worldly authority, but with the loss of the inner as well as the outer mediator. This is an ethic without ethics, a religion without salvation.

"Enlightenment rationalism" is presented as the autonomous adversary of "revealed religion." Yet it is the dependant, the cousin-german, of the *unrevealed* religion. Enlightenment rationalism can have no genesis; but it was born in the late eighteenth century. For prejudice, superstition, subjective whim, illegitimate authorities, received tradition and revealed religion, reason substitutes disinterested truth and the objective criterion of judgement, grounded on independence, on the resolution and courage to use one's own reason. *Sapere aude!*—Horace's "Dare to know!"—is made by Kant into the motto of Enlightenment: "Have courage to use your own reason." Kant made it clear that this address to the individual was not an address to the private use of reason, but to the critical intelligence, to vigilance in the public use of reason, whose freedom was bound to be restricted by "reasons" of state or church. If Enlightenment is grounded in the free use of reason, then reason is grounded in enlightened self-interest: in what a people may without coercion decree for itself.

The tentative but critical, ministering spirit of Enlightenment has been *bouleversé*: grounded in an overweening claim to absolute and universal authority, without awareness of history, language or locality, enlightened reason sweeps all particularity and peculiarity from its path. The original plea in Kant for submission of conflicting views for public adjudication has been turned into the univocal imposition of a standard, whose very formal impartiality masks its origin in a partial interest. This argument from Rousseau and Marx, that a particular (class) presents its own interests as the universal interest, when they are opposed

to the interests of other particulars (classes), has not
been dismissed with the body of Marxism. As the ruse
of reason itself, the argument has been extended and
attenuated. O reason—ambidexter implement for
effecting the irrational!

Immanuel Kant was an ardent Pietist, a follower
of that Protestant Counter-Reformation, the Reformation of the Reformation. He knew that, since
Luther, authority and scepticism keep changing places:
one person's authority is another's scepticism. Descartes drew his *voie d'examen* from Calvinism; in turn,
the French Counter-Reformation drew its fideism
from Descartes's scepticism.

When Scripture was substituted for sacerdotal-
ism by the Protestant Reformation, it was claimed that
reason had replaced superstition and worldly authority. "Subjective whim has replaced the apostolic tradition," ripostes the counter-claim. Once this exchange
has been launched, all authority is relativised, because
both sides are ultimately sceptical: the one of received
tradition, the other of human, finite knowledge. The
only way forward was to make a virtue out of the limitation: the boundaries of legitimate knowledge are
endlessly challengeable, corrigible, movable, by God,
by man, by woman. There is no rationality without

uncertain grounds, without *relativism* of authority. Relativism of authority does not establish the authority of relativism: it opens reason to new claimants.

When I claim that women's experience has been silenced by the patriarchal tradition, which represents itself spuriously as universal, from where do I speak? From women's particularity? Then how could I speak? I could only stutter. From patriarchy? Would it want to unmask itself? From sceptical faith, shaky but persistent, in critical reason? I bring the charge that reason's claim remains unrealised from that transcendent ground on which we all wager, suspended in the air.

Unrevealed religion is the progenitor of enlightened reason and of reason's offspring, postmodern relativism. Reason is protestant—it protested against abuses of the Church's authority in Germany; then it protested against what is called "superstition" in France; first, it was called the Reformation, then it was called the Enlightenment. Reason intensifies the consequent crises of authority, first by the turn to an inner, direct relation to the Author of Scripture, then by the turn to the immanent practitioner of criticism. If Luther delivers religion to the Prince, then Kant delivers the public realm to the protestant revival. Postmodern relativism is the new baroque stage of the protestant revival: reason is apparently being forced to abdicate at the combined protests of its unsatisfied petitioners.

There is one sense in which I do want to rewrite my history. Even in the earlier version of that history, feminism never offered me any help. For it fails to address the power of women as well as their powerlessness, and the response of both women and men to that power. My fulfilled love relationships have been with two younger men, both English poets and continental philosophers. I lived with one for ten years, the other for five. I consider this the period of my fifteen-year "marriage"—the kind of marriage that Kafka knew he could not have with Félice, where the singleness of each is enhanced by the communion. Feminism does not discern the beauty or the limitation of such a love in which each is equally teacher and taught, Lover and Beloved. Outsiders misconstrue the meaning of the chronological and social inequality. The woman is not the mother, the man is not the son. No *folie à deux*, the relationship has a third partner: the work. The work equalises the emotions, and enables the two submerged to surface in series of unpredictable configurations. Work is the constant carnival; words, the rhythm and pace of two, who mine undeveloped seams of the earth and share the treasure.

I suppose I thought that the third, the work, came to supplant the fourth, the world, for the younger partner, the apprentice, who is also *Meister*. In both cases, I, the older creature, have initiated the rupture, on perceiving signs of withdrawal and depression. The "beautiful soul" came to inhabit the Beloved, who, as youth, was vibrant with ambition as with poetry. I thought, mistakenly, that I had become the world, the still challenging drawback to further explorations. Feminism does not speak of the woman with the gift and power of Active Intelligence—to speak in the terms of Avicenna's angelology—who gives love and draws it to her, enabling and difficult. Tarrying with the negative, I accounted myself too bounteous and too restricting. And so, with much pain, I broke away, ending, not friendship, but the throes of erotic and ethical love.

Now I think I was wrong in this analysis. My friends continue to suffer the same agony of soul. With me or away, in other relationships or alone, the specific difficulties of each individual history are accentuated not arrested, relieved, developed or baptised.

They may have no more or less to learn, but I did, and still do. For, while those communions had their complexities, they did not display the intractability, the withdrawal of love, the refutation of shadowlands, which I now face. Matured by love, practised in the grief of its interminable exercise, I find myself back at the beginning. Is feminism able to credit that it may be better, sometimes, not to get what you want? Here is an experienced, independent, creative woman in a relationship where she has no agency, where the boundaries are drawn and redrawn by the Lover, reticent yet exacting. Neither self-effacement nor self-assertiveness, neither inexhaustible patience nor reminders of his power, will bring about what I desire. We are protestants; impatient with ourselves, outraged by others, righteous, we claim a justice that we never yield.

L'amour se révèle en se retirer. If the Lover retires too far, the light of love is extinguished and the Beloved dies; if the Lover approaches too near the Beloved, she is effaced by the love and ceases to have an independent existence. The Lovers must leave a distance, a boundary, for love: then they approach and retire so that love may suspire. This may be heard as the economics of eros; but it may also be taken as the infinite passion of faith: *Dieu se révèle en se retirer.* Love and philosophy may seem to have had the most to say, but friendship and faith have been framing and encroaching by night and by day.

This comedy is not *postmodernism*, the new baroque protestantism of the body and denigration of the mind, which would lull the senses with the rainbow of saturated hues, with the aroma of sweet herbs. Comedy is homeopathic: it cures folly by folly. Yet anarchy exposed and enjoyed presupposes a minimal just order. There are no collections of jokes associated with the Holocaust, although there are now collections of Hasidic tales of the Holocaust. Suffering can be held by laughter which is neither joyful nor bitter: the loud belly laughter, with unmoved eyes, from North Carolina; the endless sense of the mundane hilarious of one who goes to Mass every day; the gravelly laugh roused by the whimsical poetry of the incongruous in one who has damaged lungs.

• • •

I like to pass unnoticed, which is why I hope that I am not deprived of old age. I aspire to Miss Marple's persona: to be exactly as I am, decrepit nature yet supernature in one, equally alert on the damp ground and in the turbulent air. Perhaps I don't have to wait for old age for that invisible trespass and pedestrian tread, insensible of mortality and desperately mortal.

I will stay in the fray, in the revel of ideas and risk; learning, failing, wooing, grieving, trusting, working, reposing—in this sin of language and lips.